After going through 45 pages of your book, I just want to tell you --- I think I am reading one of the best books of my life...I don't want to leave it for a min and want to finish it overnite.. Its brilliant!!! Hatss Off!!! :)

SWOT, Drop And Roll

Leveraging Your Weakness Into Your Strength + 48 Other Articles

jamie smith, PE*

* Author of the #1 Amazon Bestseller, 7 Steps Out Of Wage Slavery. Over 100k Views/Month Blogger. 2x Speed World Record Co-Holder.

Published by Renegade Strategic Creative Agency, Inc.

1st Edition

Disclaimer

PREFACE

Yo – It's been an amazing experience (so far) sharing my thoughts, experiences, ideas and life with you (the reader). My hope is that this helps you find clarity, joy, laughter, empathy and a connection with myself and those around you. It is truly through these human emotional connections that we gain our greatest joys.

Please understand that the ideas in here are Very Real – Unfiltered (sometimes unedited) and are my attempt (although, at times clumsily) to understand what is going on around me. Please integrate what works, disregard what is counteractive to your intuition.

If you have any comments, I can be reached at

therenegadeinc@gmail.com or

http://twitter.com/WithOstomy

For more articles, browse https://TravelWithOstomy.com

If in the future, I am too famous to check all emails, rest assured that there will be some system in place where I am still in the loop. Yo ;)

Keep Rocking. Be AWESOME. Adventure On, Always.

Jamie

P.S. As an aside: These blog posts are placed in reverse order. This is done to build suspense. And cause it helps me understand – "Where Did It All Change?" Turns out it could have been as simple as getting rid of sugar and adding honey. But, I'll leave it to you – the reader – to make your own conclusion. Anyways, you would regardless.

Live your own life, make your own decisions. Rock On.

Table of Contents

"Strength is in control" <<
Choose Your Focus.

The other side of "Lifestyle Design"

Been right at one year living in Tijuana; haven't Been to the US in many weeks.

Overall – Shit Is Fucking AWESOME

Want to share a couple realities though – To show that it's not all rose tinted glasses

1. *Was the victim of an armed robbery in a dark alley about 2 months after moving here (had local taqueria keep an eye on me for the next month after that when I had to walk through the alley)*
2. *Was Hit by a car running a red light (I Broke 4 Bones in my hand and couldn't bend my knee properly for over 2 months – took a taxi yto the US where I limped a mile to a hotel to monitor my injuries for several days)*
3. *Witnessed a man being taken into an empty house followed by another man with a sledgehammer (Didn't Have the number for*

police >> *Or Know how to call them. We Since have solved this problem)*

4. *Had the house on lock down (All Doors and Windows locked, plus curtains drawn while we held the phone in our hands)*
5. *Regularly have to pawn the TV or/and the tablet to keep food on the table, cigarettes and coffee. (Always buy back A Week Later)*
6. *Spent 3months sleeping on a tile floor (Often in a wet blanket because I don't have a dryer, and 4 months of ice cold showers because I didn't have propane for the hot water)*

Would I Change Things???

Well Yes, obviously.

Has It Changed Me?

Yes, Without A Doubt.

So tonight, I was driving home listening to the new Slipknot Song (FUCKING CRANKING IT. YO)

When I Thought?

I Am So BADASS

I actually have to tone down my Badassness on Twitter and Social Media.

I Actually Hold Back A LOT >> LIKE A FUCK LOAD.

"Strength is in control" << Not sure if anyone else said that << But, It's What I Think about a lot.

Yo – True Strength is having Control of yourself.

So While, there is good and bad to Living Here (Because Yo, that's How Life Is)

How's It Going? Good And Bad >> No Single Point Response to a Dynamic Life

I Keep Myself in control of myself >> Or, more clearly, my response to external stimuli.

Because, While you (I) may find myself In A Shit Situation. Or A Great Situation – Claro que si

Yo – Have control of yourself and your response.

That is strength, And How You keep going >> Choose Your Focus

Manufacture urgency

Yo - Straight up.

Not sure how much longer I have

I live in a dangerous part of the city, my house doesn't have bars on it, I have to be Aware that everyone knows who I am >>

For reference, I haven't seen another white person in months (Besides one dude at the supermarket a couple weeks ago)

So Why Am I Here?

Great Question!

Why Not?

Look at the benefits >>

I've (since moving here)

1. *Released a 39 song debut album*
2. *Performed the first 10 songs from it in a 48 minute concert*
3. *Written nearly 40-50 new blog posts*
4. *Turned that into a new memoir*
5. *Taking an eBook that sold 1 copy into a #1 Amazon Bestseller*

6. *Then turned it into a 400 page paperback*
7. *Started a record label*
8. *Paid my rent, utilities and started a store with royalties from that record label*
9. *Created a publishing company (For the book and memoir)*
10. *Formed a C Corporation*
11. *Taught myself corporate law to transition that said C Corporation into a S Corporation*
12. *Made it compliant*

It's Been 5 1/2 months.

Manufacture a sense of Urgency >>

I'll Keep You posted if I Stay Here (AKA SUPER PRODUCTIVITY) or If I Go To A Different Area.

For Now, The PROS Way outweigh the Cons.

Also, Putting together 3 courses: Psychology, Rapid Language Acquisition and Basic Achievement Strategy.

I Couldn't do this ALL If I didn't have a sense of Urgency.

Take a step towards the unknown in a direction of a dream >> How's that feel?

FUCKING AWESOME?

Yes, I Know. That's What I Do basically Every Day.

It's an Addiction.

Addiction: Attraction to a feeling.

It Feels Good To live this life; I Am excited when I wake up; I FUCKING Love Mondays.

I Do Want you to feel this sensation

Feel this greatest of sensations; Feel Alive.

Yo.

7 Step Cycle of Action >> Moving Forward

Yo – Learning Is Looking at what happens

You Have the choice to Understand What You Tried To Do >> And The Reality of the situation

1. Test
2. Observe
3. Understand
4. Change

To Continue With my Theme of the *7 Step Cycle Of Action* >>

It Would Be This:

1. Open – I Was open to creating a new blog post to test things out

2. Idea – I Had an idea of how I wanted it to look (and with so many other blogs, I knew The Appearance I Wanted For it.

3. Design – I Started to design it in my mind

4. Build – I Wrote It

5. Adapt – EXACTLY Where we are right now

6. Remove – Let's See What happens and If I Can remove this problem from things I NEED TO DO [FOCUS ON]

7. Move – AKA >> Continue Moving Forward, I.E. To The next problem. Oh, There's No Problems. Well Then Make One

And That Is Your Daily Lesson on How We Operate

Adventure On >> I Do Mean It

Be BADASS >> On The Regular

FUCKING ROCK IT >> Kick The ASS Out Of Your Pursuits

CEO Mindset >> Take Charge

Yo.

"It's Actually Really Scary/Anxious-Ridden/Exhilarating"

Got Home about 3:41am last night/this morning.

Had a date >> So Following my new rule I Didn't do anything work related

No Tweets. No Checking Email. No Webdesign/Writing/Editing/Or The Like

No - I'm Just kidding. The Battery on my phone died so I couldn't do anything.

But, You see

It was on my mind

So I Got home

Plugged in the phone and waited for it to charge enough to power on

It did (while I made a cup of coffee)

Remember it was maybe 4am by this point

Turned on phone, sipped my coffee, and started writing emails

Why?

Because on December 5th the store opens and I release my memoir about the last 3 months

It's Scary

It Keeps me up (Although not just thinking about it >> But Also working on it)

And I'm wondering >> Is It Good enough (No, Let's change it). Is it the right length (Let's add more info.). Is the font right/colors right/All the minutiae >> So Many Decisions

So on December 5th you will see it. It will be live.

And then Maybe I will go to bed early HAHAHA Nah. No FUCKING Chance of that.

When one thing is finished, It's Time to move on to the next >>

In The Comments >> *What Do You think it should be called "my memoir"?*

Adventure On, Be BeBADASS, Fucking Rock It, CEO Mindset

Get Out Of The House - Get Into Living (In Reality)

You see I saw a lot of these so-called, "Lifestyle Designers" Bragging about living in Tropical Places, Drinking Fancy Drinks, Relxing 24/7...

But You see their pictures were always (Ok, Like 99%) them on a computer #FuckingLame

Hence:

<u>Living the tablet lifestyle AKA the active business owner lifestyle</u>

It Is ABSOLUTELY 100% Response to this HORRIBLE HORRIBLE trend of Avoiding Life and Skirting your dreams by building a "Lifestyle Business" that let's you sit on your couch (Or Ok, I Give it to you, your porch) and Spend All Day on the computer.

It's Why I Bought a Tablet.

... And Why I Recommend it To FUCKING EVERYONE.

GET OFF THE GOD DAMN COMPUTER.

It All started when I started looking at ways to record Skype videos...

It was Spring or so 2014... youtube'd "Record Skype calls"

AND EVERY-100%-OF-PEOPLE WERE IN LIKE a dark cave with a headset talking to people

Like, Seriously, Can we be real for one second

Do you HONESTLY Consider this communication???

:/

If you've seen SpanishCerveza.com - I Talk about how communication is Primarily Non-Verbal

So Ok, I Give It to you - Skype Video is a way better way to communicate than email, comments, ETC...

But the point is that it's not in Reality.

Connect with Reality, Get Out Of The House, Get off the God-Damn Porch.

Get A Tablet -

Get A Fucking Life -

Get Out Of The House -

Get Into Living (In Reality)

And With That Being Said,

I'm going to go for a walk.

Peace,

#FuckingRockOut #BeBADASS #AdventureOn #TakeCharge

P.S. And you CAN Record Skype Video Calls with a Tablet >> I Use the Dell Venue 8 Pro tablet running Windows 8.1. Yo ;) and I use Skype call forwarding with a US number to get business calls on my phone (no need for a Wifi Hotspot)

5 Specific Ways I save money (That could work in your country too)

1. For free haircuts, I go to local beauty school. They're Free Plus we seem to Always have fun joking around.
2. For dental, Also go to local college. Here it's UABC (the Otay Campus). I got my teeth x-rayed and checked out for 10 pesos (like 75 cents). They also do cleaning and all Dental work. I don't know the cost.
3. To save money on water, I bought a 5 gallon container (called a Garaffon) for like $7 and then a hand pump for maybe 30 pesos from Bodega Aurrera. It lasts about a week and only costs 11 pesos to fill up at the local corner store (10 pesos if you catch the truck with garaffons).
4. For cooking, I bought a small electric eye. It was Maybe 30 pesos - A Couple bucks. And we use it with the wok for all the cooking - 97% of the time that means beans, tortillas de maiz and chorizo.
5. To get from here (La Presa) to Centro, I can walk to the boulevard and get on a "school bus" Calafia and go all the way for 10 pesos (like 70 cents). If I'm doing a new route, I will take the Calafia or

Ruta (minivan) all the way until it stops - It's Typically where it starts the return trip and I learn the entire route.

Keep Fucking Rocking - In the comments, Let Me Know if there's a Specific Question You Have About saving money, living larger, or making a home in a new country on a budget.

You Can Change The Rules – Fuck It, New Game.

Let's say you are playing poker.

You get dealt two 2s and a bunch of cards that don't help In Any Conceivable Way.

What do you do???

You bluff. You see what everyone else has (Or More Clearly Is Projecting To Have). You compare the SHIT you got dealt to WHATEVER THE FUCK EVERYONE ELSE HAS (OR WHAT YOU THINK THEY HAVE).

The point???

You FUCKING GUESS, COMPARE, PROJECT, HYPOTHESIZE... Basically you Compare.

And You Panic

We'll Let's Say you instead got three Aces. (4 Would be too improbable for this Example HAHAHA)

You are Sitting Pretty – But Still You Are comparing – All that other SHIT.

Now, you Think, "how much do I bet, bluff or not??? Rope in these poor suckers for All Their Money."

And inside,

you know what happens –

You panic

Well let's go back to the two 2s Example.

YOU KNOW WHAT YOU DO???

You Fucking Change The Game To Gofish – Make 2s Wild – FUCK IT. Anything that gives you the Advantage.

But You can't Change Rules Mid-Game.

But you Can change your life

You can make the Rules

(Really You Should Have, Already)

For example, I started using profanity and write more Natural

So Fuck Playing Poker, Start Playing Life – And if you don't like the cards you're dealt. Fuck it. CHANGE THE RULES.

Yo ;)

And that's my secret . I make up the rules in my life to Win. Hope This Helps

You #Win #KickAss #TakeCharge #BeAWESOME #Adventure On

And, one more thing –

There is NO scenario where this doesn't work AND

You Have To WANT To WIN. Yo ;)

Question:

One Rule You Want to add to you life???

Interview of Mr. Jamie Smith – CEO, The Renegade Inc.

Helloooo Peeps!!!! This is your very own Ms.Kate and I am here to interview Mr. Jamie – The CEO. Ahhh!!!! The sun is too bright and it seems as if it wants to shine brightly all through the hot day... Nevertheless... Before I start I just want to throw some light on how Mr.Jamie managed to take out some time from his tight schedule.

5 days back when I was piled up with lots of emails, I saw one of his blog link and when I read it I was like — Gosh!!!! He is the one I was searching for past 6 months... He has that powerful charisma and the *'Yes I can do it'* attitude which is surely going to motivate thousands of other people all around. I contacted him and - see his generosity — he took no time to decide that yes he will open up his life in front of us... Get ready peeps!!!! It's time to read his hard life, get inspiration and feel motivated. Now read below, what he has to share with us!

So, Mr.Jamie, thank you once again and let's start -

Kate: On a scale of 1-10 how awesome do you consider yourself?

Jamie: 7, always room to improve

Kate: What is the major turning point in your life?

Jamie: I've had several moments – when I was young I was told the doctor's didn't think I would have a long-life, shortly afterwards I read an article about an actor dying of Hirschprung's at 30, intellectually I understood it was irrational – but it created a "deadline" that pushed me to have a "complete" life – like I never dreamed of old age with someone, didn't think I'd ever get married, have a family, kids, Etc... the thought of "what do I want to do for my "career", the rest of my life never really came into play – take away a family, career, kids, house – what do you have to live for??? Being a friend. So it wasn't until my late 20s I started thinking – Well Shit, what do I want? I said "Oh Fuck", I could be around for a long-time HAHAHA what do I want to do until I retire. Repeat the same engineering project; do the same routine. It wasn't until years later when I started building real lasting friends around mutual interests where I started to really change my mindset and consider – Hey, Life is pretty Fucking Awesome when you have people to have fun with. So one instance??? Nah. Several instances culminating. Learning of my friend's suicide was the prompt to continue following my dreams; I saw the alternative. So while I do a lot of cussing, and can be direct – it's because I've seen first hand and from other's experiences what happens when you compromise – it's not an option. I see no other way to live my life besides the way I am living it. Long hikes, bike rides, international travel, hours of meditation – they all have had an equal effect in shaping my beliefs, thoughts and actions. Every day when I wake up I choose to continue my life – every day is its own turning point; success or failure, mediocrity with addictions or more with clean living. I've struggled with addiction all my life – so everyday is a turning point – towards the future or the past. I know the past – the future, I'm open/curious/excited/wondering/anticipating about.

Kate: Where do you see yourself 10 years down the line?

Jamie: I don't think that way. Where do I see myself at the end of my life – and what's going to get me there. In AA, NA, DRA (Dual Recovery Anonymous), I see so many miserable people living on will power – not acting natural. When I got my bike I just naturally didn't want to drink or do drugs – I just have no desire. Maybe I'm lucky, I don't know??? To answer the question – happy and enjoying life and I'll do whatever the Fuck it takes to get there (within the law).

Kate: What if I say — You are freaking Awe—Some!!!!!!!

Jamie: Ehh. I don't think that way – You're my hero. I don't take praise well. Umm... ok. Thank you.

Kate: Should I tell the general public that here I am interviewing the leader of the 21st Century?

Jamie: I don't have any followers. I prefer just to do my own thing – never tried to fit in or felt comfortable or successful seeking approval. Never felt approved of – but made peace with that. A long time ago.

Kate: What is the one word that comes to your mind when someone says — My life is not worth!

Jamie: Really, I try to tune out everyone – you could say I live in my own world, but more accurately I work hard to focus on what brings me forward in life; I have said that I tune out criticism and praise equally – really just staying focused is a challenge enough in itself. I have learned recently however that I like people that help make my life easier.

Kate: What is your biggest asset?

Jamie: I really don't know LOL

Kate: Are you crazy?

Jamie: Crazy is a horrible choice of word. I don't label myself – it's a form of restriction. However, I can view situations as sane, insane, naturally, I have self-awareness - I can view myself, the situation rationally/objectively and confer, "whoa, what the Fuck am I doing" – but often times I need to process to understand my motives – I can get wrapped up in following my unconscious mind and act on intuition rather than my analytical mind.

Kate: If cat = dog what will be adventure = ?

Jamie: AWESOME

Kate: What do you mean by ' Making Ostomies Badass' ?

Jamie: After the ostomy, I saw several people just staying at home complaining about the symptoms (which I concur are very real). Uncover Ostomy was the 1st person, Jessica Grossman, who made it "sexy". I like the word "badass" after seeing a friend post a picture of her with the caption – "badass". I saw the picture and liked the way it made me feel about this person. I said, someone's got to do it – I already was jaded by the clean-cut, corporate, Bullshit, car salesmen, slicked hair, Bullshit suit and tie life coaching image and said Fuck it – it needs to change to be more from the heart – Fuck it (I live on disability). I have no boss to answer to, no need to sell an insincere image to feed myself – Fuck it, I'm going to use profanity and document my life (with the real scenario of failure). I'm in a unique position – 34, fixed income, no boss, who else gets the opportunity to genuinely express their frustrations, hopes, everything on their heart without having to cowtow to a single person. It's not original to me, I have a friend here who uses the phrase, "radical honesty". I dig it – it keeps me off addictions, keeps me moving forward, having fun – Fuck it. You have no clue how freeing, "radical honesty" is HAHAHA

With this question, here I end up the interview. Thank you once again Jamie for taking out few moments for us. I am sure, many of our friends will find an inspiration in you and there is nothing better than making people come out of their shells and feel motivated.

Have a good day!

It's Time to Risk It All (Some) In Life

So maybe you've dug through these posts - and you found the one line where I say I was diagnosed mentally unstable HAHAHA Look at my life - who wouldn't be. ANYWAYS.

It makes Risk/Reward all the more important.

There is a HUGE FUCKING Risk to my mental state by doing some of the things that I'm doing: traveling, meeting people, dating.

I know I have a tendency to go hypomanic or depressed when I start a relationship (depending on the person)

So I'm constantly looking at ways to mitigate this risk: I.E.:

Having people around, a sense of focus, eating corn tortillas instead of flour, reduce the sugar - increase the honey

Basically, it's a constant changing emotional state and it's risky - the Reward Has To Be FUCKING Huge for me to take a risk

I.E. I wanted to join a bike group yesterday - new group, cool ride, close to home

So I called a friend - "Hey, can you do the ride with me" "Ok" "Cool, pick you up at 6"

Mitigating risk while seeking reward

I found this article this morning:

"Five Ways To Get Anyone To Do Anything You Want" by Bruce Kasanoff

1. Make sure the other person has the ability to do what you want.

2. Offer a reward.

3. Guarantee the reward.

4. Reduce their costs.

5. Reduce their risks.

It Applies To Dating, Business - Really Any/All Aspects of Living.

The point???

It works for you too.

These principles work when you are examining a new situation you want to try:

I.E. Can you actually do it? What do you get out of it? Is the result a sure thing? How confident are you that afterwards you will get the desire outcome? Is there a better or cheaper way to get what you want? (And most importantly) Does it reduce your risks?

It's 11:01am on a Thursday - feeling good about meeting new people, exercising, riding my longest trip to date here - I'm stable, comfortable, and feeling good about the decision. It's kind of what I thought would happen - it worked out.

Question:

Is there a situation (relationship, job, friendship) that you want to try but aren't sure. Does this simple checklist help you?

A 10-Year Look Back

Been about 10 years since graduating from engineering school at Virginia Tech.

2 years steady meditation

3 years weekly therapy

Backpacked Europe 2x, Costa Rica, Peru, Canada

Passed engineering licensing exam on 1st try

Wrote and self-published a 400 page self-help/business strategy Amazon #1 Bestseller

Wrote and recorded a full length music album and performed it in concert

Lived in a little cottage at the beach for 2 years

Explored and photographer all the major parks in California

Road tripped the 101 from LA to Portland

Hiked 40-kilometers at around 15k elevation

Mountain biked in actual mountains

Designed, managed, engineered over 10 school upgrades

Part of team to be listed as groundbreaking in the San Diego Business Journal

Moved to a new country - moved farther into that new country

Ran a popular blog

Started a record label

Quit drinking, drugs

Was given a new life with a permanent ostomy

Next 10 years...

I want someone in my life to share it with (not necessarily romantic) and a child. Besides that - I think it's better to figure out together. Maybe a new album, trip to China, return to Peru, drive to Costa Rica, rent an apartment in Vienna, break $1 million with the business, travel for 6-straight months. Let's call this the anti-FUCKING- bucket list HAHAHA

In the comments:

What do you want in the next 10 years Yo ;)

Response to "If true love doesn't terrify you, you're not really getting it." #truthbomb by Danielle LaPorte

So every couple weeks or once a month, I would call her to just say hi.

Get together??

No, you're busy - sure. Talk in another month (when I have enough strength to say hi)

It's like, "Hi. How are you? Yup. Sure, oh by the way - I'm terrified of you and avoiding you because you could hurt me."

Falling for someone is by far, IMO, the scariest thing in life. It's like –

"Hi. I am aware the best situation is that I die before you and then you hurt - besides that it's basically guaranteed you are going to hurt me at some point but STILL I will be with you (knowing that eventually it will hurt me)".

And, this I why I'm 34, never been married, no kids –

FEAR. HHAHAHA

Danielle LaPorte's #TruthBombs

And one more thing — how I live with this fact:

Like the previous blog, while every relationship/experience comes with it bad/hurt/pain, it also comes with it the opposite. I think it's best to find your moments of ecstatic engagement - include the person in these moments, and use them to ride the storm/enjoy the bliss/find your peace, joy, tranquility, amongst all that is out of your control.

Because in a nutshell, you're giving control of you to someone else/the universe/God/the Divine - and that can be FUCKING terrifying. Yo ;)

"It Looks Like You Are Living The Life You Want"

Yesterday, I got a message from a family member. They said some shit like, "it looks like you are living the life you want." I wasn't sure what to say - Still am not. It's an interesting statement.

Why??

1. Am I Really? I don't know.
2. What life do I want to live? I have a clear(er) vision of it.
3. What would I change in my life? Does it matter - it IS propelling me forward and dictating my actions (to a large degree)
4. Is it REALLY something helpful to think about? Do I need to stop what I'm doing - examine my life - Say, "Yes..." something like "Yes, after dealing with a shit situation, I am loving my life" or "Not really (my contrarian streak) say - You have no clue the BULLSHIT I deal with in my life..." and then list of examples.

Really, it doesn't matter. I'm curious however what the next sentence was.

As in, "it looks like you are living the life you want" AND ".... " Maybe "I'm happy for you", "Good for you, I know you worked really FUCKING hard to get to that place" or MAYBE "I disagree with that life and I think you are making horrible choices"

I'm sensitive. I admit it. I am super hard on myself and struggle with self-limiting beliefs (that are starting to change).

I just don't know what to say if you don't say what you're thinking.

HAHAHA so sure, but it's a weird thing to say.

It's like, "wow, congratulations on picking out that shirt and putting it on"

As in, it just is what it is. I suppose I could say, "Well when you consider the alternative to living the life you want, I don't think it's viable."

Probably, at the end of the day, I am just a little bitter. HAHAHA

I constantly think: "You know when I was really going through a hard time, I never got calls, support"

But of course, I also believe that you deal with your SHIT in private before going in public - SOOOO I kinda hid while I was dealing with the height of Crohn's (unable to get out of bed, changing my diaper ever hour (or less), and on the verge of being homeless).

So how about - "Thank you for letting me be part of your life. I am aware that you have chosen to share your life - and I am honored that you let me be in it"

Maybe that is a grandiose thought - but again, it is a choice to share my life with others with the very real thought that, "Yes, I can fail." I don't have the comfort of someone providing for my financial security. Yes, I know I get disability, Yes I know I have gotten help from my family - but my dreams are very hingent on the success of what I'm doing. I REALLY have a lot riding on what I'm doing - Like, All my dreams are riding on this. Do I want to continue living the life I'm living for the rest of my life?

So just like you picked out a shirt to wear, you followed your intuition, God, the universe, whatever you follow and decided that this was the right thing to wear (or in life to do).

I suppose I felt welcome/loved/appreciated/desired/alive/ETC at some point while living in Tijuana and craved that feeling again -

But, Really

At the end of the day - much like that shirt you are wearing, I just put it on and got on with my day.

So, am I living the "life I want"

Yes, no, *somewhere in the middle.*

Real quick - I have a neighbor living with me now. What does this mean? It means, I have a whole new set of problems but also benefits. And at the end of the day, she adds more benefit to my life than problems.

Much like that -

I have a different set of problems that I live with. But they seem to suit my strengths and the benefits outweigh the cons so it just is what it is. So when a new situation comes up just say:

"Sure, why not"

Do the Right Thing

Consider the big picture

And don't think "why did I put on this green shirt"

Just put it on - and go about with your life.

Every person/situation/experience has with it good and bad -

At the end of the day is there more good than bad.

If so -

CongratuFUCKINGlations, you are living the life you want. The details don't matter too much. Yo ;)

Turn Your Weakness Into A Strength

I have a friend in a tough legal situation. I don't know the details. When I say tough, I think I am being too easy. In Reality - It's Probably A FUCKING HORRIBLE STRESS INDUCING PIECE-OF-SHIT SITUATION that FUCKING SUCKS. But I know she has a level head and I don't give her a "sorry for your problems" because I know she doesn't want sympathy. What she wants, I'm not sure - I am sure when she knows (or already does) she will take action or ask someone.

The Point???

I'll share a quote. First sentence from "For the New Intellectuals" by Ayn Rand. (This is basically a treatise of her philosophy of Objectivism that she examined in her novels. It's also the only sentence I read before closing the book and getting on with my Shit. Why - You'll See).

"When man, a business corporation or an entire society is approaching bankruptcy, there are two courses that those involved can follow: they can evade the reality of their situation and act on a frantic, blind, range-of-the-moment expediency – not daring to look ahead, wishing no one would name the truth, yet desperately hoping that someone will save them somehow – or they can identify the situation, check their premises, discover their hidden assets and start rebuilding."

The point?

When Shit Happens - you have a couple choices:

1. Be a bitch (not in the feminist way - but in the way you just complain and do nothing about it)
2. Use a clear, calm head to figure out what the Fuck You Can Do, Want To Do, Is the Best Action -

Basically, What the Fuck Are You Going To Do About It.

Yo - as you can see by the headline. I shit into a bag. It's something I have to face everyday and for the rest of my life. It can and does debilitate people in fear, shame, ETC... You Get the point.

The way I live with it (and Have a FUCKING super happy life???)

I turned what is a Shit (pun) situation into a strength. I thought calmly about it and realize that it gives me "cred" in a small group of people not bitching about their life - but actively creating a better one (and future).

Yo - When I get crap from other ostomates (and it does happen), I smile. Yo. I smile at the people who roll over - never leave their house - bitch about their day. It gives me time to get even farther ahead and reduces the competition.

Yo - Everyday, I can look at this ostomy and say "Sigh... my life is hard, it sucks" or say, "Fuck YEAH. This is my ticket to my future/dreams/goals/ETC..."

You get the point -

So next time you get in a SHIT situation - or if you're in one now -

Yo:

1. Figure out how to leverage it into a strength
2. Be clear on what response you want and tailor your actions towards it

Because, you may not know clearly exactly what is going to bring you happiness but bitching at home never worked for me.

Take Action. Vibe With Life. Feel Your Emotions. Live It. Love It.

And Just go with it (yo, it could be what propels you to your dreams.)

Look you're not the best, but maybe you can bring on the best AKA get a mentor

I have so far worked on this project - book, race, music, ETC - solo (basically) for several years now. Yes, that's YEARS. Yo ;) A lot of time in the grand scheme of my life.

Couple observations:

You need to believe in your abilities, have confidence and not get overwhelmed thinking of the future

Whatever you want to do - someone has already done it and has a SHIT load of experience i.e. don't reinvent the wheel by yourself

By far - the business has progressed the fastest when I have a mentor (someone I trust that gives me confidence in my abilities and knows the shit I haven't even realized about; shit I'm not even aware of that should worry me - Yo, they already have guidance on that shit.

You have no idea how relieving it is to (like Allstate) "Be In Good Hands".

AKA I got help with what I'm trying to do.

Yo, I saw this interview with the rapper Naz on NPR (yo, I only get a couple channels).

In it, he describes his philosophy:

I Did It My Way

He says it's like Frank Sinatra. I guess it's an old song.

The point:

You can (and need to) do things "Your Way" but that doesn't mean you want to go alone.

Yo, you will see your life, relationships, business, the whole kit-and-caboodle (probably spelled wrong) when you find someone who can advise you. Really, like I said, running in circles - sure, whatever getting lots of experience.

But, yo for success -

You need someone else's experience too. Because SHIT you could be so FUCKING CLOSE to success, but like Tolstoy's beggar, be looking the wrong direction. Perhaps you are sitting on your gold???

Yo, there's value in someone who has done things, has experience, in saying -

"Yo, you have your ass where you head should be."

Or, something like that.

I'm saying - yo, get a mentor.

Because, yo in life coaching it's said that you have all the answers within you, but yo that's wrong - you have what you want to do in you (and again "I did it my way"). But, maybe you're not seeing your best success because you're going alone.

African proverb: You go faster by yourself but farther with a team.

Yo, find someone whose already gone that way and is willing to walk it more or at least guide you and **FUCKING ROCK IT, YO.**

YOU CAN DO IT.

But, more apropos - you can do it (with a mentor)!!

An Open Letter to Ms. Kate About "Achieving"

Dear Ms. Kate,

I thought about what you said. I don't think there's anything special (inherently) about me. I wrote this to explain how I live my life. It's not luck but something else, as you'll find out. Great Job so Far!!

An Open Letter to Ms. Kate

You know how I set two world records, self-published a #1 bestseller, got in top 10% of timeshare sales, released a 39 song debut album, got my engineering license before turning 30, managed so many projects, ETC? It's midnight on a Friday and we're working. It's not dedication, determination or the like. It's because it's fun. We keep it light; we innovate; push the envelope. Always, I have lived my life my way. It keeps life exciting. At the end of the day, I can lay down and be proud of what I've done; everything I touch has my signature: fun, professional, new. It's not a secret but I keep life fun and that desire to keep having fun is what drives me to keep going when a normal, sane person would have been done. I love my life and maintain a sense of excitement for what's ahead. I live on my terms, and, in general, live a fun, quiet life. I ask, "why not" instead of saying, "no" or "can't". I don't live with limits. I work too hard, live too hard, love too hard. There's no ends and everything I do is a means to a better future. I constantly am suprising myself with what is possible. I never see problems but opportunities, and I have fun with what I do, and on a Friday at midnight I'm working aka still having fun.

Jamie

How I ran a sub-30 minute 5km with 0 training

Ok so with music, writing, etc now you have decided to move to sports? :o Cool!!!!!! / Ms. Kate

These are my 7 keys to how a ran a sub-30 minute 5k with 0 training, smoking a pack a day and drinking a pot of coffee a day. Really, this Shit is easy. It's All in your mind. These principles are based on mu understanding of cognitive behavioral therapy psychology and Eastern philosophy (Buddhism).

Not an end but a means

Yo, you think when you cross the finish line it's the end, but really it's just a step to something. For me, it's when I confirmed my lessons in the book and blog work in real life, are repeatable and I can claim that they can work for anyone. I kept this in mind, and was thinking, the whole race,

"I can't wait to tell people I ran an entire 5k race"

Yo, even when a red traffic light stopped us, I kept jgging in place. Fuck no, I'm not going to quit with so much at stake.

Yo, know WHAT you get out of the race - FUCK It, maybe just to brag, launch a business, IDK, just find something that this race will get you closer to.

Compelling Why

This is 100% related to #1. I am launching books, music, and right now a new service to help people with sports performance.

Why???

Because I want to be happy.

Why???

Because I want someone special in my life and I know happy people attract happy people. Yo. Just how it is.

Don't Go 100%

Yo, it's really tempting to go all out. Get this Shit over with. But, that's the mistake 1st time and inexperienced runners make. Yo, I ran at 50-60%, sometimes at 70%. It's not an exact science, but I find the key is to always keep that "Burst" in reserve. If you feel like you're starting to lose your ability to have a fast sprint burst, you're running too fast. Hint: There's cameras at the end of the race. You want to give 100% then, but for the race, keep it at 50-70% of your max.

Be Aware

So how do you know how fast you're going???

Be Aware. I'm not a big fan of meditation (in general, I prefer action to peace of mind), however, it's an excellent way to cultivate present-time awareness i.e. mindfulness. Just stop whatever you are doing and focus on your breath. I like to think of a metronome when I meditate. It's rhythmic, it's consistent, and the tempo it keeps (in my mind) shows me how fast my "monkey mind" is going.

So while I was running, I would naturally drift into thinking about "my why", "how's my partner doing", "oh, look, something shiny" and would have to bring back my mind to, "how fast am I going. Whoa too fast, slow down a bit."

The key is to be aware of how fast you are running.

Have a partner (teammate)

Like life, it's just more fun with a partner. However, this doesn't mean you run together. But before the event, after the race, it's Fucking Awesome to have someone to prepare and celebrate with. Being a proud member of Equipo Extremoso (Extreme team), we met before the race, walked and talked to get ready, and then through the race (she's way faster), I was excited to share the race victory with her. I feel like a big part of sticking with this is to have a partner. Pyschology Today had an article a couple weeks ago about how "Couples who sweat together, stay together".

A little honey

This is my secret food that propels me in sports and race. I'm not a nutrition specialist, but it's my understanding that it provides a quick burst of energy (and I think mental clarity), lasts a long time, and doesn't lead to a crash. I think it's considered a slow-carb i.e. it doesn't spike your glycemic index (what makes you crash and want to take a nap an hour after drinking a soda). Because you don't get the crash, it's not something you really get addicted to. No dependency. Plus it Fucking tastes Awesome!!!

Race in reverse

All of these are centered around one thing - racing in reverse. Start slow (warm up, get in the groove, cultivate awareness), know afterwards what doors are going to open up because you completed the race (what is this a means to), don't spike yourself on energy drinks (but slow-carbs, also eat something like pasta 3 hours before the event).

The key to all of this is to know what do I get out of this, go at a pace where you can keep that quick burst a suprise. And yo, most important. When you do all these things. Remember there's one more thing: Smile -

keep having fun with it. There's cameras at the end - make sure you can show your best. Look, I did it. It's not Fucking Hard. And, It was fun.

If you want, more 1-on-1, purchase a Sports Performance Package and let's find a race for you or get you ready for your next event.

Big surprise and changes coming soon

After a Fucking Awesome call with Ashley of

www.yoursuperawesomelife.com

some Fucking BIG changes are coming...

Stay Mother Fucking Tuned!!! Yo ;)

Your life doesn't flash before your eyes AKA "Huh."

When you get hit by a car, it is a weird experience.

One moment you're running to recharge your phone before the show, next minute, you cross the intersection

Redlight, ok, cross walk sign is on, no cars coming, Go!

Get almost to the other side and look to the left.

"Huh."

Is all you think.

"Weird", normally the car is passing by my side but this time it's right next to me.

So, you're life doesn't flash, there's no thought but a simple, "Huh."

And, you think - "This is new."

That's about it LOL Not really FUCKING Exciting HAHAHA

You hear a thud, realize, that as much as you try to control your life - in a moment, you have ZERO control of your body.

You simultaneously think, "Ok, get up and check your body" and "Did the guy stop, can I get his info."

Ok, get up, bounce a little on your feet - "Ok, nothing broken." Guys long gone by now, quite possibly speeding up to cover his ass after VERY Clearly Making His Problem (Phone, Drunk, Reckless, Out of Control, Who knows) - Making whatever is his problem now is your problem.

And, you don't even have a say in it. Basically you get a problem dumped on you, without any concern for if you're ready, if you want it, if it's fair to you.

So what do you do???

Say, "FUCK It, change of plans. Walk AKA hobble half a mile or so to meet your friend. Basically, whatever is the most important thing before is probably the most important thing after.

So what changes???

Really, not much. Your life continues, broken hand-sprained knee and all. Life doesn't go on pause. The responsibilities you had before, are still there.

So what is the best advice I can give???

Hmm. If you live or die, doesn't matter to the universe. You are replaceable to the universe. But, not to your loved ones. Be smart - get insurance, have all your bases covered before hand (i.e. I had a week's worth of ostomy supplies on me), have your life in order.

I work from home. I can keep working.

Life goes on. Basically, this is new.

Ok - best advice.

Here we go -

Have one thing in your life that gives you a sense of urgency. And have one thing in the future that you look forward to. Yes, sure seeing a loved one sounds nice. But, I mean Something BADASS - like snowboard in Mammoth, mountain biking in Baja, these are a couple of mine.

Yo be BADASS, when you get hit by a car in life - bounce back, check everything is basically cool, and keep The FUCK on, and keep that vision of the future - 'Cause Yo -

You'ld be suprised how much BULLSHIT you can take if you have a clear vision of one thing in the future that FUCKING Pumps YOU UP. Yo ;)

and how am I doing???

HAHAHA No estoy muerto. HAHAHA I'm not dead. Gracias a Dios. So I think it's funny ;)

Depression & happiness are how you perceive the future

Disclaimer: This blog was written a couple days before I was hit by a car. It could have been lost. It is the last unpublished blog in my 8 days 2 blogs a day streak, and is Blog #52. Please enjoy. If you have a topic you want me to write about send me a message at juanderer21@hotmail.com. I try to answer all emails but if you don't get a response, keep an eye on the blog!!! ;) Buen dia, Enjoy!!!

Depression and happiness are two sides of the same coin - the future.

It's all about how you see the future, I.E. do you look forward to it or dread it.

You see the future is not necessarily 10 years away - 5 minutes away is also the future. It depends where you're focused. What future are you looking at, your like FUCKING 5 year plan, or the future when you get into the office, or the future next time you see someone.

What future event are you looking at???

Living with a chronic illness, creates, or can, create depression. You look at the future with dread and every time you think of the future you're scared.

So what do you do???

Out of sight, out of mind - in a sense. I.e. don't think about it so much, don't talk about it (you see I barely if ever mention the word ostomy in here) instead choose to focus on actions a person (like me) can take to improve their future.

Because truly it's about how you (and me) see the future.

You have these thoughts, programmed from when you were young, and when you have one your body releases the appropriate chemical. The steps are thought first and then the chemical release. But first, it truly starts with the belief or thought.

What are your thoughts about the future. You see that's where your emotions, feelings, basically everything lies.

So you can FUCKING meditate to create mindfulness (present-time awareness) and deny the future, or you can start taking actions to make your future better.

Truly It's A FUCKING GREAT IDEA

Start Making Action Real Today

Take charge of your life,

That pretty girl that flirts with you - ask her out. Either way she responds, you are taking control of your future.

And once you do that - the future starts to look pretty FUCKING BRIGHT. Yo ;)

I just write from the heart, thats all i do!

Instead of asking for handouts, I believe in working hard and smart for what you want. I used all of my strength to write this book. In it are practical, actionable strategies to achieve the most in life. How do I know it works? I live it everyday, and every moment. Look at my life as an example. "Do not explain your philosophy. Embody it." Epictetus. Life is change and like Mackievelle explains in 'The Prince' the key to success is learning to adapt.How??? By the end of the book you will know. But one step is to create a very specific handwritten compelling vision of where you see yourself in the future. This book is for anyone with the audacity to live life on their terms, as they see fit and without apologies.

At 8:50 PM I was hit in the crosswalk by a car running a red light. The driver did not stop and no one got information. The car was going 30-40 mph, I estimate. I got up, checked, nothing broken. Walked a quarter mile to meet my friend at the show. Made him attend and afterwards took a taxi to the US border where I called an ambulance to check me out. After spending all my savings fighting Crohn's plus getting the ostomy, I barely survive financially each month on the little I get from disability. That plus book sales and individual brainstorming sessions are how I survive.I do not want a handout and instead am selling preorders of the next edition which over 70 pages of extra material at a limited time discount of $109.

Register yourselves right here and get your copies -
 http://bit.ly/RegisterYourselfToday

The age of missing information* AKA the big why questions

*not to be confused with the Bill McKibben book but along similiar lines

Ok, someone posts a status update that they are at their favorite place. Ugh don't really know much, sure "like it" but Now I'm wondering a lot about the why's.

Why do you like that place, why out of every place in the world is that your favorite place. Because really it's not chance - i.e.

What's the story???

I.e. maybe it's the first place you kissed someone, your dad took you there when you were young, you want to buy a house and can see the land from there

Whatever the reason, Why??? What is the story???

I am genuinely curious.

All day long I get status updates from various networks - at my favorite restaurant, at my favorite place, with my favorite person, I want to start knowing WHY.

I'm genuinely curious.

I don't know you if I don't know your Why's.

Why is it so important you climb mountains???

There's a saying, "the only Zen you find at the top of a mountain is what you brought there" Yo, some SHIT like that. So what I'm saying is, "who is taking the pictures of you", "why is it so important you climb mountains".

Because yo, in Psychology Today they talked about an old study that showed that you can truly have like 5 people in your life with the most intimate emotional connection - i.e. everyone else in your life is on the outside wondering why, cheering you on (but not knowing, truly, why).

Like, I want to like you, in some deep level I really want to care about you, but if I'm just "liking" your status updates and not learning the why, then I'm on the outside looking in - and like when you go window shopping, it's nice to look in but you don't stay for long.

Let me in. Let me ask why. Let me learn more. So probably I'm prying, but yo, it's because I want to care. It's like you show up at the end of a party and everyone's cheering for one person. What's the first thing you do??? You turn to someone and say, "Hey, what's going on???" I want to cheer for this person to, but I'm curious, WHY.

Yo, if you want to make deeper connections, ask why.

"Breathe. Breathe in the air. Don't be afraid to care" / Pink Floyd

Then when you ask, "how can I help", you aren't coming from need, you are coming from caring(love) and that's NEVER a bad thing. Yo.

Whatever you look for in life, you find

Yo, think you're a horrible person - cool, trust me, you'll find evidence

Think you're a great person, cool, you'll find evidence

Yo, basically the point is that you have these beliefs and they cause you to have feelings and actions and ask questions

These questions will be like - Am I a horrible person??? it's really your belief that "Hey, I'm a horrible person" then you looking for evidence. Which you'll find.

So WHAT'S THE FUCKING POINT???

GLAD YOU ASKED

Look at your beliefs before you start looking for evidence to prove them.

I.e. change your belief and change what you're looking for, change what you find.

This is basically Cognitive-Behavioral Therapy in a nutshell.

I got into this SHIT in like 2010 when I was looking for answers in my life: bad anxiety, couldn't date, couldn't open up or be truthful (scared of rejection or SOME SHIT LIKE THAT).

So I started really talking with this girl and she said she was taking a CBT course and described like the basic ideas - like experience + knowledge = wisdom (it would become the basis/framework) of my book.

So, how do you change your belief.

Repetition, questioning, talking about it, being open about it.

"What you resist persists"

Dude, so FUCKING gratifying/liberating/therapeutic to write a book - I wrote it for two people - one specific person to read and for my piece of mind. He bought one, I felt understood. FUCKING WIN-WIN.

Hence, why I found and created this CBT BOOK - instead of writing for one person, I choose a topic that is already proven to be "the premier therapy for depression" by Psychology Today. And, now I'm adapting it towards one person, in particular, to be a customer - but this time, it's cheap, it's accessible, it's repeatable as a business model, and it's most important written by a source with credibility to the material.

So yo, I have this belief that it will sell.

I look for evidence -

I disregard the low, if any, sales so far and instead find evidence in the popularity of the UK course. I.e. two pieces of evidence - one good(for), one bad(against) - but, because I have this belief I REALLY DON'T CARE ABOUT THE BAD - LIKE TRULY, IT'S NOT THAT I IGNORE IT, I DON'T CARE, I DON'T EVEN IGNORE IT, I JUST LIKE DON'T CARE LOL. It's out of alignment with my belief structure so I don't give it any weight, instead I weigh the evidence that it's already been proven to sell well MUCH HIGHER.

Yo, in a nutshell, what you look or you find, and what doesn't match your belief doesn't matter - it carries no weight and is filtered out through the lens of your belief autobiography(set of beliefs we have)

People will eventually take the easiest route

I have a friend here, he's a compromiser - i.e. he expects people will help him when he gets in a jam

Ran out of money - it's cool, his sister has a good job

No electricity, it's cool - extension cord to the neighbor's house.

Is it a BAD THING???

No, not necessarily - I suppose he has a good heart

Is it someone I want to spend my time with???

Sure, but in limited dosages

You see his habits become my habits and most likely vice-versa. I suppose.

When I first met him he said pretty quickly, he was an adult orphan - a weird term. He explained he grew up with parents but now they were dead.

Ok, "I'm sorry" - thinking, "why's he playing the sympathy card so soon". I didn't reveal my own struggles.

I started to pick up little things where he wasn't really taking charge of his life - girlfriend bought computer, now suster will bail him out when he runs out of money.
Again, nice guy but are these habits I want - do I want to start depending, or thinking, it's ok if I mess up - someone will bail me out.

I KEEP SEEING THIS SCENARIO, EVERYONE DEPENDENT ON ANOTHER, BUT DEFINETLY MANY EXCEPTIONS.

So what happens - a person doesn't do the hard work of working though a relationship issue and walks away, a person loses electricity because they don't pay after spending hundreds on tattoos, ETC.

Basically, you think you're life sucks because you don't have easy outs - YO, NOT A MOTHER FUCKING BAD THING.

On a long-enough time line someone with the option of taking the easy road out, will. Don't be that person, proactively remove/get rid of the thoughts/options that you have an easy way out. It may seem that today you can "tough" it out - but willpower, like a clenched fit, eventually gives out.

Yo, don't compromise, <u>don't think there's an easy way around hard work + smart action</u>, and be careful hanging around people who behave this way - they will teach you both directly and indirectly their ways.

 If you're going to compromise, do it in the beginning - then it's not a compromise it's maybe a smart move. Yo ;)

68

Are you selling unicycles to paraplegics?

Ok, I know your mental image, yo, I got it too.

A paraplegic riding a unicycle.

Could happen, but is it common???

Imagine your business is selling unicycles - are you going after that crowd. Yo, obviously not.

What's the point???

I see more and more people with ideas of what they want to sell rather than what their customers want to buy.

For example, you're an English teacher in México. Your students don't want lots of individual classes where they pay each time. Yo, it sucks paying. Times that sucking times each class and pretty soon the suck factor increases to a point where passive behavior starts, i.e. not showing up, cancelling last minute, "being busy".

Yo, so what do you do???

Two options:

As needed help for people who just want at a lesson per time

An English course guaranteed to get someone up to a level where they can communicate, i.e. get a job in English

From experience, I don't want to pay for a unicycle if I can't ride it. Yo, I want something that is going to help me with what I need: perhaps to travel, perhaps to have conversations with pretty gals, perhaps to open up business opportunities. Yo, I DON'T NEED TO BE FLUENT, I DON'T WANT TO INVEST TIME IN SOMETHING NOT GETTING ME TOWARDS MY DREAM.

WHY???

As, I keep saying - Yo, it's about how you feel.

Feels bad to give money or something I don't want, i.e. every time I give money, I'm reminded of this fact.

If I don't FEEL good, I'm not going to put my heart into it, i.e. I'm not going to stick with it.

I.e. I'm going to stop and you're going to say,

"I'm confused, I guess he didn't really want a unicycle"

So yo, the solution:

Give help, as needed, or

a course that is proven to work, i.e. repeatable.

People want two things:

Money and

pussy

Take one of those two things away and you better have a better replacement.

I.e. if you're charging for a service, make sure it's repeatable (i.e. worked for x and will work for y) and it will put people in a better position AFTER taking it then before, and also don't push what position it will put people in - They know.

Yo, you can spend all our time pushing unicycles on paraplegics, yo, or you can work SMART and work less with higher results.

Yo, my math tutor and I have a good arrangement. She was super stuck on the basics, so I spent an hour and taught her my tricks. No, see you tomorrow. No, lessons all week (and pay me each time). Nope, she was stuck on something, we spent one hour solving it. I am easy to get a hold of if she needs another lesson (like a 1-hour crash course) but my goal is, for whatever reason she wants to learn, to give my best to teach her that skill. Yo, so advertise, it's great, but don't push your product or idea - instead ask,

Today, what do you need to learn.

I.e. Where can I help you that you can't help yourself. Advertise and let people come to you. Trust me, this is better for everyone.

Does this make sense??? Tell me in the comments!! Yo;D

How I started spending more money, living more, on the same amount of money ?

So yo, like three weeks ago the internet went out at home

HOLY FUCKING SHIT, right??? For someone who basically lives on and does FUCKING everything on the internet, yo, This is a big deal

I started going to a local cafe (actually several Instagram.com/withostomy) and thought, FUCK ME, this is going to get expensive QUICK, yo

But a strange thing happened (is happening), I haven't run out of money - No, in fact, I have more money then really I ever have

Why???

Or, more like - HOW???

Yo, so in the beginning, I went to the cafe, pulled up my bank statement for last month or maybe two months and made a list of every automatic transaction. Then, called and either cancelled or put on hold everything that wasn't making me money (renegadeincorporated.com - Volusion store, cool, good idea, not inanially paying for itself - YO, it truly us like 100% FUCKING the ROI) so I put that tore on hold (down to like $10/month), did same with Shopify store, cancelled lots of little like $3-10 business services that maybe made me feel cool but didn't directly make money.

Found a new home for T-Rex (my foster cat), Yo, cat food adds up quick.

And, Yo, started looking at internet cafes and coffee shops to run business, plus being out of the house, I have to buy food. Thank God for panaderias (bakeries) where I can get pan integral (whole wheat rolls) for like 35 cents (whole wheat more filing so you eat less.

Found a coffee shop near Centro where I can get an Americano (espresso+water) plus Texas toast for like $2. Yo, it's filing and yes, it adds up, but not as quickly as $10 internet services.

So somehow, I'm kicking ass this month, I get paid in a couple days, have plenty of money to last and yo, Thank God, haven't had to pawn anything to get by

So, yo, in a recap, print out your bank statement, create an itemized list, address each money drain/expenditure individually. Get out and enjoy life, in a financially responsible way - and yo, you'll fond too, yo, truly there is an abundance of things you can do on not much money and still, maybe even more, enjoy life, because you're not so stressed about money.

Yo, it's an abundant life when you don't spend money on lots of small SHIT that doesn't get you towards your means.

How tutoring one math student taught me 10 things about business + life

Today, I made like 130 pesos as a math tutor.

NOT REALLY A BIG DEAL - *or, is it???*

I am proving that it's not necessarily about following your passion but your skill set,

Now, as a reader of this blog, you know that I constantly stress vibing with life

So, yo, today I did just that.

I got a tutor request a couple days ago via universitytutor.com.

Math help

Like the equivalent of middle school math.

So, what I did was take it.

Figured, I'd figure it out - I mean, yo, I got a degree in engineering, I KNOW MATH LOL!!!

But, also,

I need credibility in business.

Yo, let's kill two stones with one bird.

I want to travel, I need income, I need business credibility - so I leveraged this one class to address all these needs.

Yo, I am using my skill set to develop another one - business.

I could look at the 10 years as an engineer as time not spent learning business, or leverage that time spent in a new direction - i.e. I may have changed careers, but it's FUCKING stupid to throw out the baby in the bathwater, i.e, what from that career gives me a competitive advantage now, what skills translate, what can I STILL FUCKING use, but maybe in a new way.

So, hence, I can spend that time doing math to become a tutor to learn first hand more about business.

I NEED experience, what from my past experiences gives me credibility - i.e. where am I an expert where people will pay money.

So, yo, just in one hour, I learned several things about business.

10 quick lessons

I can be a viable business

It feels FUCKING weird to get paid, but I like the feeling

If you charge, people will work harder, and

She told me how much my fee was, I had no clue(it's not a bad thing), before contacting me she knew how much I charge (even though I didn't)

Being responsible for my future (but knowing I can handle it) is both empowering and freeing

You think I would go celebrate with a big dinner or blow the money, but instead I don't know I get paid again so I had 1 tamale, a small coffee, and some noodles (like $1.70) for late night

I have wondered if ESL teacher's could teach other subjects - yes, with my limited vocabulary, we could still communicate

It feels REALLY FUCKING COOL to see someone learn and make progress, and it can happen quicker than you think in 1-on-1

Everyone here thinks teaching English is best, but I made more hourly teaching math

Don't try to make friends with your students, Yo, it's business - a financial transaction has occurred, maybe be pleasant, but keep that professional distance

Cool, if this helps you - Tell me in the comments. Yo

Lighten up Yo

Yo, learn to have fun with life

Dude, NONE of us gets out alive HAHAHA

Dude, just take things as they come, learn to lighten up, stop complaining, stop whining about how other people are affecting you

You - yes, You - learn how to laugh at life. Something good happens: OK COOL LOL. Something bad happens: OK COOL LOL

Yo, just have faith in your future, believe you are capable without any outside help (Yo, rely on YOU, Yo)

Don't be dependent on people, don't stress what other people do so much

TRULY, THIS IS NOT FUCKING ROCKET SCIENCE, JUST FUCKING LIGHTEN UP

Yo, don't give advice to people, mind your own business, and just

Let go

Take action

Accept what happens with a smile

Because, Yo

WHAT'S THE WORSE THAT CAN HAPPEN???

YOU DIE???

PFFFF... Not that bad.

But do you actually LIVE

Yo, lighten up, and next time say FUCK IT, SURE, WHY NOT???

When, life gives you lemon's say,

FUCK IT, OK COOL LOL

Dude, just let go, take that action that's going to make you look at yourself and say, "Well whatever"

People will like you more, you'll get more pussy, when you Just Let Go and Laugh at life.

Lighten up, Yo.

Love or fear or to love fear

Yo, there's basically two emotions everything can be distilled to:

Yo, is it out of love

Yo, or is it out of fear

Basically, anger for example is wanting love but not receiving it - wanting to control love and being upset when you don't get it - Yo, TRULY, LOVE, FEAR AND CONTROL REVOLVE THE UNIVERSE

Well... if you know me, you know I like to offer another option, a fresh take/perspective

Perhaps... loving fear... AKA TO BE IN LOVE WITH FEAR/THE UNKNOWN/WHAT'S OUT OF YOUR CONTROL

If you read this regular, you know my philosophy in a nutshell is simply:

Vibe with life

I.e. let go of controlling the external by creating a long term vision for yourself and being smart with different strategies to get there

For example, a job is a means, that company you want to start is a means to an end, that girl you want to marry is a means to the end

Like some Bruce Less shit - you focus too much on the means and controlling it, you lose the big picture SHIT

I could complain, I'm not making much money with this - yo like 100k internet hits but jut a little money.

But, instead (ok, sometimes I complain a little), I more focus on the big picture and am building one means (that I think is best for me) to get to my BIG PICTURE/VISION/GOAL/ maybe dreams, I don't know

I LOVE FEAR

I love not knowing the future

I LOVE THE FEELING THAT I AM IN CHARGE OF MY LIFE (NOT DEPENDENT ON ANYONE, PERHAPS CUSTOMERS) AND IF I SINK OR SWIM IS UP TO ME

Yo, SUCCESS OR FAILURE????

My choice, yo. It's FUCKING scary, it's fearful to put yourself out there (to have your heart on your sleeve) AND I FUCKING LOVE IT.

So, yes, there is FEAR, like a shit load, but yo, I can swim, I can a little more each day.

Also something weird happens when you take control of your life - everything out of your control suddenly seems like, *"Fuck it, whatever"*, doesn't stress me so much.

So,

it's about control, and

it's about fear, and

it's about LOVE

And we're all wrapped up in it.

And If you think you are in control, avoiding fear, embracing love - YO, YOU ARE MISSING LIFE

I.e. this morning I went to Centro to have a quiet coffee and do some work.

Reality: first coffee shop was closed, second didn't have internet, and my quiet morning included a parade of fire trucks down the main drag - of course, with their lights blaring!!!
LOL

So I said, Fuck it, whatever, walked to another coffee shop, and along the way got a quesadilla for lunch, the Xolos (local soccer team is playing) and wrote a blog.

So Yo, I don't know what strategies, I'll use for the future - it's scary as all FUCK

And, I love it - having life (not me) out of my control

So, yo, Fuck it, let go, vibe to this (go WITH the moment, not against) and start to LOVE FEAR - TO BE IN LOVE WITH IT

It maybe the key to success, I don't know, but MOTHER FUCKING REGARDLESS, IT'S FUN AS FUCK

And, I love the fear, yo. The future may be unknown, but I'm not

"To know others is wisdom. To know yourself is enlightenment" / Buddha or some SHIT like that!!! Yo.

Embrace curiosity and love fear. LOL!!!

My backstory

I beat a terminal illness.

It's a happy story.

I flew to South America as a last ditch effort to find a cure. I did, in a sense, and also I didn't.

It wasn't long term.

I spent the next two years between moving, traveling and being bed ridden.

With what little strength I had, I typed a like 326 page memoir/business plan/life coaching strategy.

I had tried for years to find a cure in San Diego, but like that show *House*, the doctors at the hospital would meet and couldn't find one. I had no hope in San Diego. I barely made it to Virginia.

I had been waiting on traveling money from my tax return - I had no other money left and was homeless at this point. I had left México in the middle of the night when I ran out of money and had been living on the streets because I knew I could get food.

On a sidenote, I went to church the most I ever did in my life because they would feed me.

But above that, there's really no help, not unless you have no one and want to spend years digging yourself out - Yo, this is one time I say to use family, friends to escape because it's nearly impossible to do on your own and the system is broken/ineffective.

So,

A frantic drive to Houston to see family and an overnight flight to Washington, DC, I was at my parents house.

A week later my insides basically gave up.

Emergency surgery later I found my cure, I had so been looking for.

But, it didn't make me happy.

I was given a choice: be stuck at home for the rest of my life or have a bag of shit taped to my stomach.

The first choice meant continuing a life of hospital stays, waiting for the next emergency - or, maybe for the first time in my life - a chance at normality so many people either take for granted or wish they had.

After, just breaking down emotionally at the thought of a colostomy bag permanently (followed by an extended stay in a mental hospital followed by a week in a group home because I was afraid how people would react), I started living a *normal* life.

I tried to get a job, wanted to want to buy a house, tried visualizing having a family, but nothing made me feel content.

I reached out to old friends and tried to find one of my only childhood friends.

He's buried in his families cemetery, I don't know the location. His father may be buried there too. Both freshly dug.

I talked a life coach into getting me to buy a plane ticket to return home - Tijuana, México.

A couple weeks later or so, I packed a carry-on with a borrowed copy of *Eat, Pray Love* from the library and several hours later got a ride to the border.

I know the ideas and theories in the book I wrote are hard to understand so I spend my time - refining, learning, explaining, writing.

I've learned since that my theories on extroverts is correct (it's about where you get your energy),

Agree with Danielle La Porte that the way you feel is most important and

Rationalize with Machiavelli that adaptation is a big key to success.

I wish I had a choice how I wanted my life to be -

The first 30 years were centered around finding a cure,

The next 30 on using it as a strength???

I'm not following my passion (exclusively), I'm following my opportunity.

It could be a weaknesses but I'm leveraging my experience and present situation is a strength to teach other people.

"Only the educated are free" / Epictetus

How the ice lady got me as a loyal customer

First, off, yo - ice AKA en Spanish is called "Hielo", it's also similar in name to what the drug dealers sell in Centro - this is not what I buy

What I'm talking about is ice frozen with tang and salsa (hot sauce).

She comes around like everyday, normally like 11am, today around 9am.

She asked or maybe I just said today... no, no quiero... ok., 3 por 12(pesos).

She left and returned with three small bags.

Basically,

It's just a small bag filled with water, tang and hot sauce (<u>NOT FUCKING ROCKET SCIENCE</u>) an they cost me like 30 cents each.

Why do I buy them???

Because,

I care about my health LOL!!! More specifically how I feel. I.e. I take the ice, put in a plastic (BPA free) canteen with honey, chamoy and a little extra hot sauce ;) and then fill it all up with water. Voilà, I got my "energy" drink for the day - it saves me money having to buy SHIT while I'm out, it stays cool longer, it's refreshing as all FUCK, so for whatever reason, I normally buy a couple and keep them stockpiled in the freezer.

How did she get me so dedicated as a customer???

She came around everyday - first, 1054089258 times I said, "Nope", ok maybe like FUCKING 7 times

One day, I said, "ok, one" or maybe I saw someone with one and figured if they liked it, I'ld try it - I'm hazy on the details.

Well,

After that one, I figured out what I could do with it, hey Yo, not really digging popsicle but hey, it has a different value to me!!!

I don't like dealing with her, it's all business, so the interactions are short (don't know her story, don't need to, just want to buy from her)

So yeah, found out like a week ago sometimes these bags go for 10 pesos each, so I really am getting a deal

Review:

I saw her everyday before trying one
Limited interaction with her
She came to me
I found an alternate value/use to what she was doing - i.e. her way isn't work or me, but I found a way that did

Now, I look forward to when she comes around, it's not that I can't make it, but Yo, really not how I want to spend my time.

The viable alternatives aren't appealing,

I feel like I'm getting a deal with her,

She's consistent

On a side note, in college, when I ran *Jamie's Bologna Sandwich Connection*, I had a special, <u>The Special K</u> meal, named because it was a sandwich and soda from Kroger (called Special K). It took off because, I found out later, Special K is the name if a recreational party drug. People looked t my special, and said, "Huh??? Really???" Then typically would buy one. Where I made the majority of my money, people like to feel they are getting a deal and people are curious when detail are vague.

Passion business or just paying the bills

The thing I wonder now after several months is it better to make money or love your job

It's a little controversial in these circles

But I'm a bigger fan of making money rather than running a passion business that runs you into the ground financially

Here me out

Everyone wants to have their dream job because it will make them feel happy

Well you know it's not bad to have a roof over your head, electricity, running water

So you know, in my business, towards the end of the month (most of my income is disability), I have to start making choices:

Feed the cat or me, or eat the cat and solve both problems???

Pawn the tablet or TV???

<u>These are the real choices I make.</u>

I never had these situations when I was an employee, working as an engineer

Do what makes you the most money, it says in *The Richest Man In Babylon.*

Sounds good, practical, but what if that makes you miserable???

<u>False question, Yo.</u>

It may make you feel discontent, but miserable - that word is thrown around too MOTHER FUCKING haphazardly.

I stay focused on my dreams, a job is a means - and work to examine different means to get there.

Because you can have your cake and eat it too, but maybe not the perfect flavor at first. I.e. you may have to work a job you don't love to get you where you want to go.

And this week, I learned it takes like 3 MOTHER FUCKING years to get the business really going.

Yo, you want lights, electricity, running water in those 3 years???

Jump in,

learn to swim,

but yo don't put yourself in a position to drown.

You my love your job, but your going to suck at it in the beginning because it's new. Yo, plan, how am I going to survive those three years while I get it up and going.

Yo, make the most money possible, find some fun social hobbies, get laid occasionally, and don't mortgage your house before you can afford a new one. Yo ;D

Yo. Focus on your dreams, and like me, dig in for the long haul. Because you're going to be fighting a while before you really start to make more than the job your working now.

And me, yes, I collect disability, like FUCKING $1542 a month, so once I break $700/month in my business I start to lose my disability benefits - So,Yo, it's a real issue to me

Comfort or Happiness???

Lights at home or love???

Now or never???

Success or failure???

Yo, fight smart. Yo;D

6 brilliant lessons from Zona Norte about business and life

Spent a couple hours this morning walking Zona Norte

Here's a couple FUCKING INTERESTING observations, Yo

For the record my reasons (this will help you understand my mindset)

I wanted:

A) A new battery for my smartphone

B) To practice talking to girls

Observations:

I love to tell people what I want

I kept asking people for a battery and showing my phone. Two people took the time to ask me - "Why donyou WANT" I spent time talking to these people, one person, even led me around for like 20+ FUCKING minutes to different shops, street vendors looking for a battery. Now, of course, In had the thought, " OK COOL Sure, this is Where I get murdered LOL!!! But yo Istill went align because I was (a) curious (b) thought he may show me something new (c) I could talk to him (d) he wasn't pushy about selling something to me, more to get me what I wanted (a battery). HHAHA Henpunched the telephone booth in frustration after like the 5th battery dead end. Dude, this guy FUCKING wanted to get me a battery, Yo.

Everyone wants one of two things: Money and Pussy

Zona Norte is where traditionally American men go to get Mexican women. Yo, it's maybe true but it's also a hotbed for hustling. I went because they have a sobrerueda (street market) where Infigured I'd get cheap SHIT!!! Long story, short, turns out It's mostly SHIT people buy in the US for cheap and mark-up to the Mexican people. Yo, it's people hustling but not where the average Mexican goes to get SHUT aka it's not the solution to the average person's problem, AKA no high sales so while cheaper than retail, can't bargain there, not the best place to get a deal. Business lesson: I didn't feel like I could bargain or it's a deal, I kept looking for a better price or the perfect product.

I had two moments where I considered paying someone, Legitimately

Woman asked me if I wanted a blowjob for $100 pesos or $10, I don't recall LOL I thought, I guess would be nice, not what I'm looking for, you're attractive, just laughed said, "I don't know" and kept walking HAHAHA

After I was shown around to all these places for a phone, I told my "Impromptu guide" what do you want. He replied , "What does everyone want?" I replied, "Money or Pussy". He said, "say that again". I did and kinda blushed. Told him, I couldn't help him with the second. He gave me the whole, I just walked you all around what did you expect. I gave him a pack of cigarettes and asked me where I could find him if (possibly) when I needed him again. Always be looking head. Yo ;D

Just cause you got it, doesn't mean you flaunt it, i.e. don't reveal too much

Sounds wrong, but the women show too much. Doesn't leave anything (much) to the imagination. I am more attracted to the curves of a woman under her clothes than necessarily seeing them. Yo, it's the imagination of what it looks like, what he looks like without clothing that drives me crazy!!! Don't reveal too much, keep your hand secret, but let people know there's something FUCKING AWESOME in your hand AKA make people curious about you, be drawn to you. I like to figure things out, make me work just a little bit to figure out what you're hiding - And make me pay for it (to know). I'm more curious and drawn to what you're hiding then what you're showing. Let me visualize in my imagination how this could help me - you are showing, when I as a potential customer, want to figure out.

Be positioned so you are the first person see and then be direct with your offer to leave an impression

The girl who offered me the blowjob was on a small bench before a person gets to the main hub. While, I didn't take her up on it, it made me think. You see the thing is - she was offering before I got tired of the offers - it was new, it was fresh, and obviously it left an impression.

I had to pass the same gal numerous times before saying anything (making contact)

I kept going by like the same corner where this girl was working. She never said anything to me, maybe the CHCHCH that's said when you walk by, but I don't think anything. After like the 3rd or 4th time FUCKING seeing her and her ntbgiving me the time of day. I stopped, looked at her, in the eye, and said, "Eres Bonita. Buena dial" (You are beautiful. Hope you have a good day). She just looked at me smiled, nodded, and that was it. Damn it does she not want my business, did I just get rejected, was she not interested. Again, refer to #2, I wasn't making it clear I had something she wanted - she wasn't paying time with me. Smart FUCKING business women, if you ask me.

So basically,

Reveal a little so people know that you are hiding or holding back something FUCKING LIFE CHANGING, don't tell people how much until the end when you demand it, make someone else's problem your FYCKING #1 priority and have your actions match that, when you ask for payment DEMAND IT, have a place or way where people know they can reach you in the future

One more thing,

Yo, and I saw a girl that looks just like my celebrity crush, Mayrin Villanueva that is really on my mind (so don't feel like you have to be an original - copy someone well liked that people want to be with, Yo, be A viable Alternative). In audition to the other things. Yo, tell me how it goes in the comments.

Hope you get a happy ending with this story HAHAHA

Living the tablet lifestyle AKA the active business owner lifestyle

Creating the tablet lifestyle AKA the active business owner lifestyle gear:

1. Dell Venue 8 Pro

In the taxis (calafias or rutas) I can write blog posts, easy to check mail at coffeeshops, lightweight so always on me, easy to pack up and travel around with, great battery life, I don't use a Bluetooth mouse so it can be tough to navigate and limited capability but easy to type on and makes me super portable plus I don't have time where I want to work or have an idea inwant to get down (writing this at Los Perrones in Zona Rio, Tijuana, Mexico while eating lunch - can't do that with a laptop or smartphone)

2. Samsung Reverb smartphone

Probably be better here to have a smartphone with a chip as the phone services reequire chips, but it's super easy to record vines, quickly respond to Facebook messages and post tweets without having to get onto those services - again it's all about Focus Yo;D I can Facebook message without having to get on Facebook and get sucked into how many likes and newsfeed

3. Alcatel dumb phone on Telcel network

Free 5 minute phone calls to three people, normally the service is like 30 cents per minute (if used under 200 pesos a month), text messages are expensive but easy (WhatsApp is convenient but again, easy to get sucked into)

4. Gateway low-end laptop

Keep it at home, mostly for music - recording - and playing, I have Netflix so I watch Suits or Necessary Roughness while I'm working from home for ideas on the TV through a HDMI connection

Purpose:

Maximize focus on business AKA means to my dream, minimize focus on things outside of my control

Other things:

I use internet cafes to post blogs, edit website, ETC...(prefer at home but internet's down plus typically I only buy an hour or half-an-hour and FUCKING fly through my work quickly)

The thrill of the rush of life in fast motion

So what's this about??? *The thrill of the rush of live in fast motion*

Yo, just because you think your surroundings are slow, tranquil, quiet - doesn't mean you have to be that way (Ok FUCKING all the time)

Yo, develop a sense of urgency

Yo, someone wants to take your job

Yo, someone wants to build a product that will make yours obsolete

Yo, you have a competitor, even if you don't see them or think you're safe

"Believe that someone is working 24 hours a day against you" / Mark Cuban or some SHIT like that

Yo two things:

Someone is working 24 hours a day against you

Your time on earth is limited, are you satisfied you've "done your life's work"

Live everyday like it's your last because it very easily could be. Yo.

Yo when you lay down in bed do you think, *"Thank you God, I'm ready. I hope to have tomorrow, but if not I think I'm done."*

Yo, there's a philosophy, don't go to sleep if you have things unfinished. It's ok, it creates a sense of urgency, I FUCKING suppose. But for me, I give my 100% and hope if I go tonight, it's cool, Yo, there's nothing unsaid, nothing undone that matters, I beat my competitors - But most importantly

MOST MOTHER FUCKING IMPORTANTLY

I have left something that people will see, my mark, my ideas, my business will continue, indefinitely

You know what's FUCKING cool about having a book on Amazon (Actually there's like FUCKING 7), is that even when I'm dead, shot into outer space, I will live forever in my works

To quote again,

"Truth is in things, not words" / Herman Melville

My truth, my life truth, will never die.

I only have ___ days on earth. God, I hope it's a Lot, of course, but it's basically out of my control.

Rather, than trying to control it -

Yo, check this, I'll live forever in my works

So, Yes, when I lay my MOTHER FUCKING head on the pillow, I smile

"God, if you take me tonight. Yo, it's cool. No worries."

Yo, and that's how, in part, you develop that sense of urgency that propels you forward in life, where maybe you beat your competitors, maybe you reach your potential. I DON'T KNOW

But, you sure learn, that Hard Work (Plus Smart Action), helps you sleep better, live more each day, and find peace.

Yo, and that's Some real SHIT. YO ;D

Shy Extroverts

So Yo there's a misconception - introvert likes solitude, extrovert likes people.

FUCKING WRONG YO

It's where you get your power from.

Yo - Check this SHIT

Basically, an extrovert gets their power - feels recharged - when they're around people. Doesn't mean they interact, they are boisterous, No - Just being around people fills their LOVE TANK, YO (Look into The 5 Love Languages) so basically that quality time, or some SHIT, like that makes them feel recharged. So yeah, Check This, you can be Shy & Extroverted.

How do I know???

You FUCKING GUESSED IT. Yo I'm one of them. HAHHA That should surprise nobody.

I LOVE BEING AROUND PEOPLE, YO.

But check this - I'm not interested in where you're from, what you do for a living, your big dream you love to talk about (But not do anything about -

Ok, not fair, some people). No, I love the quiet, peaceful moments Shared laughing, enjoying a quiet coffee, a peaceful hike, an aggressive bike ride. So yeah, maybe I'm Shy, I tend to think *I just don't want to be drawn into your drama HAHAHA*

I dig my life, Yo, it's taken a lot of hard work to get here. Yo, I would like to enjoy my time spent with you. So, no, I don't want to talk about where I came from (Washington, DC , for the record), what I do for a living (disability, book and music sales, consulting) or really the same about you - for work I like to talk about strategies to get you to a means (how to buy a house, how to setup a business, how to overcome _____).

So yeah, I'm a Shy introvert, and yes, like Every FUCKING day, I have the thought,

"I'll never get married"

"I'll never have children"

"I'll never have friends"

"I'll never be able to flirt with a girl"

Yo, but they're just thoughts. I don't stress so much my thoughts but instead my dream and strategies to get there.

So go ahead and label me a "Shy Extrovert" I'll FUCKING wear that crown proud. And, yo, if you want to Talk about something that means something to me - Yo, You'll discover, *I'm not really SO SHY.* YO;)

So how does this help you???

HMMM... Don't feed into labels, or stress the labels you put on yourself. <u>THEY'RE JUST IDEAS.</u>

"Truth is in things, not words" /Herman Melville

Yo, don't be drawn into words, be drawn into doing things. FUCK the label or word it gives you. YO. ;)

Everyone's on their own life track

Everyone's on their own life track - so Yo

don't talk SHIT,

LEAVE PEOPLE ALONE,

FOCUS ON YOURSELF,

ASK HOW,

DON'T EXPLAIN WHY.

I like it when people explain more what they can do, rather then why they do it, or when they ask me how do I do it or they can do it.

I support people that have BEEN THROUGH SHIT and have made the conscious choice to rise above it.

I have a professional friend, who basically lived the life of an orphan - dad disappeared, mom died young. It's interesting, I'm curious about her story - but I'd rather have her write a little bit about it then give a long - poor me speech. I hear them, I don't CARE. I too could give a poor me speech - but for what??? FUCKING SYMPATHY.

I get it - You've been through SHIT. CONGRATU-FUCKING-LATIONS, Welcome to the human condition. Yo.

We all have dreams and disappointments; I choose to focus on the first.

So how do I focus on my dreams???

Easy,

I don't focus on my disappointments - and

I don't stress other people's disappointments (Really I don't even listen to other people's dreams/ unless maybe we're in a relationship because then our lives are going in the same direction).

So what's the point of this???

Dude, focus on yourself. I don't care your dreams - Yo, don't concern me.

But If, you think I can help you figure out, test, analyze one means to get there - I'll happily spend hours working with you.

So yo, want a baby??? *Think buying a house will get you closer - perhaps stability, consistency, an investment for your future and your child's future. COOL. Let's talk about how to get you the best house, how to negotiate, how to research different areas, land values.*

But yo, I don't need to know the dream, I just help with analyzing and strategizing individual means. FYI a baby is a dream: a house is a means to that dream.

Why do I like to analyze and create the how???

Cause I FUCKING ENJOY IT

But also,

"You make enough other people's dreams come true and yours is bound to come true" something like that

So yo, While I Don't Really give a shit about your dream (<u>because I try just to stay focused on mine</u>) - I will bend over backwards to discuss strategies on how to arrive there.

Yo, you are driving. You stop and ask for directions. You tell them WHY you need to get there??? No, of course not. Just "Yo, I'm lost. How do I get there???"

My response, "Sure, take a right at the big oak tree, third house on the right." or the like

Yo, time is valuable, be wise with how you use others. And when you're lost, people love sharing knowledge, feel free to ask - "How do I get there???"

Because, yo, I don't care why, but maybe I know the way.

And in a nutshell, that's how my business works.

Directions.

2 Big Secret Questions I ask myself

These are the 2 Big Secret Questions I ask myself

1. Now or never?

Yo, if I don't take action now , I will never get this moment back. it doesn't mean being impulsive/rash/hasty - but in this moment how can I leverage this towards my dream.

I mean, in life, we are given a series of moments, I don't *FUCKING* understand the past, I have a vision of the future but I'm not so fixed to it, and this moment, how can I keep my eyes on my future and Leverage This moment to propel me towards it.

You either see the world as

a problem holding you back or

as different means to get to your perfect/ideal future.

There's nothing wrong with you, have faith, build your trust, let go of the need to control.

Controlling the exterior means we lack basic internal controls -

stay composed,

consider the big picture,

consider the greatness you are building for the future.

Always be building the foundation stronger - but with an eye on the future erection that will be placed in it.

> *"If you have built castles in the sky. Let not your dreams go to waste; Just build the foundations under them." / Thoreau*

2. Success or failure?

Yo, I know what it takes to be a failure. Nothing. I mean staying in bed, sorry for yourself. What does it take it be a success??? FUCK IF I KNOW HAHHA But, if failure is when you do nothing, success possibly is the opposite. I teach SMART Action: An acronym for Start Making Action Real Today. It's FUCKING SCARY as shit to take action - It's Not, What if I fail??? But FUCK ME, what If I succeed??? What if my dream comes true and I'm still miserable. What If I can't handle the fame??? The money???

Yo, don't stress it.

The person tomorrow will be more well equipped to handle it:

Wiser, stronger, more experienced.

Let go of the need to control,

take a step today,

get comfortable with the emotion of fear -

FEEL LIVE, LIVE IT, LOVE IT,

Don't lose your curiosity that propels you in life.

I am driven by pain. It's part of who I am. I fear losing that pain, that fuel, that desire. Well FUCK IT, I learn not to stress it. Maybe I lose it, maybe I keep it, maybe it beats me up inside until I am the shell of, a shriveled man living in FEAR, Afraid to leave the house HAHAHA Beats me

> *"Don't ask questions without an answer" / Buddha*

I don't know the answer, So I don't ask the question - I Focus on where I want to be, and think

"Hmmm... what can I do this moment to get me there, without being irrational, impulsive, destructive"

So yes, in this moment, and every moment we have a choice:

Will we be a success or failure??? And while there's no answer, there's a moment to do something about it, this moment. But again, don't let it get to you, eat you up inside,

Think,

release,

move.

Tomorrow's not promised but this moment is because you're still alive

Yo, take advantage of that. Yo ;D

Kindred Spirits

Kindred spirits: as a relationship is just "friendship on fire", I think sweating together is accomplishing/overcoming/beating something together, it's that shared bond+experience that makes people so strong together,

"kindred spirits" : this is different than a soul mate but not necessarily , mutually exclusive - I don't know what the definition of a soul mate is , besides a person whom can touch you on a spiritual plane, but it's not becessarily that you both have the same connection or attachment to each other.

Where soul mates CAN SUCK as they tear you apart, a kindred spirit reminds you that you're not FUCKING alone; in the middle of the night when you're staring at the wall shaking from fear and anticipation/expectancy of the future, a kindred spirit will remind you that you're not alone;

Although we may live and die alone, we are not unique (in our experiences).

So why did God make so many people on earth???

Because we may not agree or be drawn to our neighbor as a kindred spirit, there's like 7,999, 999, 999 other people with experiences, and most likely, almost 100 FUCKING PERCENT, there's one other person with a shared experience.

So when you are in bed alone, shaking, staring at the wall, remember you're not alone, you're not alone.

Keep the search, question what you find, and hold dear in your heart those kindred spirits that keep you sane when you're soul mate rips you apart.

They both serve a function.

And when will you know when you find your kindred spirit.

I don't know...

But,

"Eyes are windows to the soul"

You'll know. ;D

And you know What's *FUCKING AWESOME* About a kindred spirit?

There will be so much SHIT you disagree on, But This Strong connection, means - FUCK IT, it's worth the blood, sweat and tears to make it work, cause the bond that grows(instantly grew) is stronger than any possible difference.

Strongest people in my life are those I've shared a tough (Hiking, biking) Experience with.

Question:

What´s an experience that has brought you closer than you can describe to someone?

Depression - when it doesn't matter what other people think, the only person's opinion that you care about is your own - and it's a pretty SHIT OPINION.

Depression - when it doesn't matter what other people, the only person's opinion that you care about us your own - and it's a pretty SHIT OPINION.

So yeah, Robin Williams, GREAT, the world loves him, but in his eyes, a failure, another attempt at sobriety down the drain. Perhaps we have this idea of sobriety all backwards - Clearly he was self-medicating through alcohol(As on the record I do through tobacco) - Maybe It's Not the worst thing. I've often thought that Probably a good beer(or 10) would help me release the interior thoughts I have.

"Alcohol reveals what sobriety conceals"

So FUCK YOU AA, 12-Step Programs, Anything That teach that there's some inherent flaw With The Perfection that You Are.

So Perhaps instead of looking at "alcoholics", "drug addicts", Heaven forbid "Smokers", as some social-pariah in need of fixing - Practice Forgiveness, Then A Heavy Dosage OF Living-Kindness.

There's Nothing Wrong With you.

Stop thinking that you're some inherently awful person that needs to practice some form of self-imposed abstinence and start enjoying, and living your life, flaws and all - Proud, and with the mentality, *Fuck You, I Won't do what you tell me.*

Live your life as you so choose fit.

And Robin, It's too late now, but live your life authentic - We Never got to see the real person, the person behind the laughs, characters, comedy - The Real, genuine, authentic, person that at one point loved to read stories to his kids, not in a made-up, funny voice, but in a genuine + caring sense. The real Robin Williams, would we(the collective) like and approve of him??? I don't know.

Look, *if people, don't like you, perhaps It's because you let the wrong people Judge you.*

"I am, as I am: hideous, or handsome, depends on who is made judge" / Herman Melville

Don't judge yourself. Yo;D

CBT (Cognitive Behavioral Therapy) connects beliefs-thoughts-actions

CBT (Cognitive Behavioral Therapy) connects beliefs-thoughts-actions (Refer to course for more information http://www.slideshare.net/jasmith6/cbt-course-renegade-inc)

Today, I find myself complaining:

I have to go to the ATM, it's a 4-hour trek.*

*me wanting sympathy to advance some mental objective

Another way to look at it is:

Thank you Dear God, I Have FUCKING MONEY to withdraw, and, sure, I'm healthy enough for a 4-hr, mostly bus+taxi trip. Yo 😊 <-Sure, no sympathy, but another way to look at the same coin. Yo;D

Thought:

I have no clients, no one needs me

Alternative:

In this moment, I have the choice and opportunity to do something about that.

> *"Truth is in things, and not words."* / Herman Melville

Don't stress about the life you're living - It Will change, the choice - Do you let life dictate your Future or do you create it through Smart&Hard work. Do you even now where You're Going in life??? Maybe that's What you should focus on in this moment - I Tell Everyone I Work with to write down their perfect life (and then don't look at it for like 6-months to maybe 10-years).

Plant a Seed in your subconscious mind.

Water it with hope, faith, belief in yourself, hard work, Smart action

"Start Making Action Real Today" AKA live a S.M.A.R.T. Life. Yo;D

And don't worry what other people think - men can be hard critics and soft supporters of the same thing.

"I am, as I am. Whether hideous, or handsome, depends on who is made judge." / Herman Melville

QUESTION:

Who Have you wrongly made the judge of you (your character, lifestyle, decisions)???

Because, Yo, I'm not communicating In A Way You Understand

Throughout time... yeah, whatever, I probably already lost you on that 1st part of the sentence...

WHY???

Because, Yo, I'm not communicating In A Way You Understand - You've Heard This Sentence before, Its Passe, not to mention dry, and brings you back to History Class (Which I Personally Enjoyed - But today don't want to hear/Write while sitting At Rosarito pizza enjoying pizza a la pierda, the view, and An Afternoon Working at the beach) VAMOS A LA PLAYA MOTHER FUCKER O O. 😊

Today's Lesson is on communication also Why Don't I give a Shit about 99% (exaggeration Yo) of your praise or criticism. It's because you are speaking Mother Fucking Swahili And I Speak Spanish. I Can't Understand You.

I Am Looking For People to speak to me like a man, you are speaking Like You're Talking To A Woman.

HUH???

"Men want to be needed, women want to be cherished" / John Gray, Men Are From Mars, Women Are From Venus [Yeah, I'm Well Read MOTHER FUCKER ☺ *]*

The point is that I am putting out a bid (*The Relationship Cure*, John Guttmann) [<-See What I mean] and your polite Refusal because "You're Good" - Is A Dagger In my manhood (maybe too graphic and weird Mental Image) -> A Dagger in my Pride, Sense of self And Value As A Member of the male race.

I'm Sure You Have GREAT INTENTIONS - Sure, Ok, Great. But the point is You're Talking In A Different Language.

AND THAT SHIT IS FRUSTRATING

So Instead Of Spending My Time Writing An Explanation (and Trust Me, 1 Key To Happiness Is not Having To Explain Yourself To Anyone)

I'm Going to write a vaguely (or overtly aggressive-passive Blog Post)

Because obviously, I can Not Understand the Words coming out of your mouth (Paraphrased From the movie Rush Hour)

Yo, When You're Talking to A Swahilian, Speak Swahili, A Latino Espanol.

Yo, You Get It And I Cherish Your Feedback And You As A Person

Just Go Get 'em Tiger - and you YO If you need anything "Let Me Know"

Cheers!!!-Jamie 😄

"The Soft Bigotry of Low Expectations" AKA Why you think So Little, Yo ;)

"Men feel cherished when they are needed. Women feel cherished when they are loved."/ John Gray, Men Are From Mars, Women Are From Venus

Wrote a book. Response = great job, its awesome. I didn't care, ok, maybe just a little.

Book hit #1. Response=Wow, that's AWESOME!!! I cared a little (more just shocked)

Book on Barnes&Noble. Response=I'm so proud. Me= I don't care.

WHY???

Am I an ungrateful ASSHOLE???

Yeah maybe, I wonder about that.

But Also -

I Know What I am capable of already. I view myself as capable and worth a Lot. A FUCK LOAD.

So I don't care what other people think - I tune out the criticism and praise; but, I always listen to Feedback and work to make the product as friendly, usable and efficient as possible for the customers.

I don't have my ego involved. You can say I am proud of you - Don't care. But say I love what you created and it makes me proud, smile, and know I'm on the right Track. Rather criticism from a honest critic than praise.

Yo - I Don't Count the praise, but the book sales and money in my bank account. Yo, praise is free - the surest sign of approval is a purchase!!! 😜

"Vote with your wallet"

I wrote the book, it got praise, no one bought it, I ended up homeless. Yo.

So Call me an ASSHOLE - But from experience, what I'm doing is not a surprise to me, I know my worth and If you want to praise or criticize - Yo, Do It with your wallet. Yo, at the end of the day - It's not the praise or criticism but the Benjamin's in my bank account that make me smile.

Yo, and if you want to say Anything - how about???

...

"How did you do it??? " <- Because Yo I will spend hours explaining for free at no charge if you show any Interest. Yo.

And, the view I have of myself -

#1 Book: "Sure, I would expect nothing Less From You." Yo.

Cheers!!!-jamie 😄

"You don't tell a cactus, it's green. Why? Because it already knows"
Spanish proverb (I don't know - maybe. Yo 😜)

Question:

What Makes you tick??? Yo ;)

My Philosophy AKA Vibe With Life + Why I Don't Like Life Coaches

Yo - I have Been thinking??? Why Don't I Like Lifecoaches.

Is it Because they just care if you pay (I hired a Lifecoach - had 3 sessions (majorly FUCKED Me up - AKA Anxiety Went through the FUCKING ROOF), I stopped after 3 Sessions - Didn't NEED That Shit. Got an Email From Said Lifecoach. Something like, "You signed up for 6 Sessions and only did and paid for 3" You KNOW FUCK You - Not "Hey, Congratulations On Learning to Lifecoach Yourself, So Happy You Don't NEED My Services Anymore, You Are Going To Do Great Things" no - Its Was, "Pay Me More, You NEED Me".

Dude, LIFECOACHING AND THAT SHIT, Is A FUCKING Crutch and an Addiction - In Some Ways, A VERY Expensive Addiction. I Saw A Therapist, Pyschologist, Here In TJ. She Told me, Maybe One Session. And You Know, That's What happened. She gave me this little assignment - Write down the pros&cons to the situation/choice/decision, You Know, ETC... I Did ... Didn't need her Help After That. Just Needed a New Tool For The Ol'

TOOLBOX. She Was, Maybe Not Happy, But I didn't Get a FUCKING Email - Yo, You Need More Help, Yo, Your Need More Sessions, No - We FUCKING Knocked It Out in One Session - 45 Minutes. Done. Fucking, Piece Of Cake.

So What Is my philosophy that Has Gotten Me out of Therapy/Life Coaching BULLSHIT. Sure - It's Simple:

Just Vibe To It

Be Clear in your head what you want - I Tell People Write down you perfect life - no Detail Too Small, then Visualize Living It - FEEL THE Emotion Of Living, Smell It, Breathe It, Embody It, Yo. ;)

Then In The Moment, be aware of this vision but Focus on Your Present Time Feeling. Learn To Get comfortable FEELING. Yes, I Joke that I Teach Men How to Feel. But It is the basis of my life, of what I Do, of everything.

I Thought I was a Radical, When I Started developing it, this, in like early-mid 2011 but then I Read/ Or Was Introduced to the Firestarter Session by Danielle La Porte and Yeah, FUCK YEAH, I'm Not the only one thinking This. And For the Record, like myself, Her Background is in Business - And IT Makes All the FUCKING Difference in the World to Start From that mindset before getting into Spirituality/Lifecoaching/ You Know What I mean. Basically, Start From Reality and work your way backwards-forwards-sideways. Yo, Its All About the Feeling(s).

Feel Life.

Live It/Life.

Be Aware (Present Time Feeling Awareness)

And Then

Vibe With it

Know Where You're going - and in the moment, think, "How The FUCK Can I use this to get me closer/To my vision" - Yo Learn to

Vibe With it(Life)

In Business, In Your Personal Life, In You Pursuits, In Your Failures(Perceived), In Everything -

Dance With Live, Make Love(Fuck It) Hard, Be With it (Vibe To it)

Yo - Goals Are a means to control Life (which doesn't FUCKING Work - and Not How this SHIT Really FUCKING Flies)

Instead of creating external controls on the variables outside your control - Go With The Flow

Yo, Go With The Rhythm, Go With The Momentary Feeling, Breathe Slowly, Run With Control, Live HOWEVER The FUCK You Choose - And Most Important

Whatever The FUCK Happens:

Just (MOTHER FUCKING) Vibe To it.

Yo;)

Cheers!!!-jamie:D

Question:

What's Something Outside Your Control that You Are Trying to control?!! Yo - Let it Go&Vibe To This. Yo;)

I don't want to be a rockstar - i want the feeling that it would give me, i.e. freedom, to be able to travel, ETC....

I don't want to be a rockstar - i want the feeling that it would give me, i.e. freedom, to be able to travel, respect, admiration, the girl of my dreams. being a rockstar, or business owner is a means, what i want is the feeling that it would/does bring.

i suspect that you want to be a model for a feeling that it would create, money, presitge, ETC... (I don't care, not my business why) - but What I am saying is there are several roads to the same destination. I.E. Figure out what Feeling you WANT (Happy, Successful, Secure, ETC... Again, Its your business and I Don't Pry) - and look at different ways to get there.

I want to have the option to live in the tropics - I want to have options of what to do in my life. I want to Feel Free. I see running a business coaching, producing music, engineering (my education + background) getting me there.

Once, you are clear on what FEELING you Truly Want - Believe You can achieve it. It sounds easy, but Truly Success Is In Your Mindset; I created this course to help people, in your situation get over the mental blocks that Really Are The True Deterrent from your success (And were mine) [See Attachment]. **STAY POSTED FOR THIS**

Look, The only thing stopping you from achieving is knowing what Feeling you want, Believing You Can Achieve It (It Really is - Talk to people already living this life, there no different than you - and Probably your better in ways than them), And Having Faith that somehow it will work out (Or You'll be Dead and It won't matter anyways LOL!!!). And For FUCK's Sake - Make your breaks, make your Luck, Break Down the FUCKING Door and announce , "I'm Here, And I've Come to FUCKING Kickass and Model - And No one is going to stop me" I'll tell you that you can do it, but Tell It To Yourself. Its all about internal motivation.

Cheers!!! -jamie:D And I'm going to post this on the blog - I Really believe in helping one at a time but sharing what works so that it can help others (Your identity is safe)

Question:

What FEELING Do You FUCKING Crave In Your Bones??? Yo ;)

Email To a business Colleague(2) - When You Make a mistake Offer, at least, to FUCKING do something

If you're starting a "passion" business, you're going to be Horrible At It In the beginning - It's New, You Don't Know WTFUCK You Are Doing - You're Going To Make Mistakes (FUCKING Fact of Life) -

This Is How I Respond When I Fuck Up (Even If Its Unintentional aka Don't FUCKING Blame Your Client, Take Responsibility And Do Some ACtion That Not Necessarily Fixes The Problem (WHICH MAY BE IN THE PAST) But Shows That HEY -

Yes, THEY ARE YOUR CLIENT, BUT THEY'RE ALSO A MOTHER FUCKING HUMAN BEING WITH REAL EMOTIONS, FEELINGS, DREAMS, FEARS,

ASPIRATIONS, INHIBITIONS AND LIVES OUTSIDE OF THE TINY AMOUNT OF TIME SPENT WORKING TOGETHER.

So Here Is the Email I Sent To Someone <-For The Record, I FUCKING Hate Revealing My Emotions - But Sometimes You Have TO Make An Emotional connection if you want someone to Listen. Also For The Record, A Picture Of You Crying in the bathtub is FUCKING BRILLIANT TO GETTING SOMEONE TO DO WHAT YOU WANT. Yo - FUCKING RULES OF THE GAME, HOW IT FUCKING WORKS IN REALITY. :

I made a mistake at work in 2010. I was supposed to submit a project or email but didn't. I got an email from the architect, _____ of _____ - She was upset that the submittal didn't come in. I told her I never got the email with the request. She replied with something like the date and time of the email. I searched through the deleted folder and Yes, Did find that email. Still I didn't remember seeing it. I asked around our office what to do - As She was clearly upset. Sue, our office manager, told me to write her a letter - but also to give her some action to show that it was not just empty words. I found an envelope of company stationary, and wrote her a personal apology and told her that as a show of my sincerity want to treat her to lunch. I then got in my car and drove to the architecture firm and hand delivered it to the receptionist to give to her. I never asked her about, we never talked about it, but as I was getting ready to leave engineering, we were working n a project together. It was a job walk about 2 or so hours before my flight to Lima, Peru. I didn't really have time. But, I went anyways, we did the job walk, and then when I was leaving she said something and touched me on the shoulder. That's it. You know, that's a sign that a person cares about you. I knew she got it, and although she never gave me a thank you, I can look back on that action and smile. I Wish You Well As you Start Your Journey, And When you run into _____-'s, remember that they have Feelings and sometimes just the small act of offering lunch and hand delivering an apology card can make all the difference. It May Be a Business You are Running, But It revolves around people - and while my dream is not to run a business - I See It as a means of propulsion towards What I really want.

Cheers!!! -jamie:D

QUESTION:

What do you do, not if, But When you FUCK Up??? Yo ;)

Email To a business Colleague(1) Maybe Its Me - I've Dealt Now with several businesses spawned <-Great Word

Email to a business colleague :

Maybe Its Me - I've Dealt Now with several businesses spawned <-Great Word/Influenced/Somehow Associated with _____.

Great Business Appearance, Great 1st Impression - But Not really digging their business fundamentals.

I Keep getting this over-riding persuasion that the business functions for THEIR Benefit, Not They Benefit The Client. Take It As you will - But no one will listen to me (Which is A. O.K. with me) but you Actually Have a Bull

Horn. Stand On Your Soap Box. It may be "_____" sure - Something Like That - But its basic Business Fundamentals, I Don't Get it.

Cheers!!! -jamie:D 10 years experience running multi-millioin dollar projects, winner of six figure design projects, ETC... AKA COnfused. Yo ;)

QUESTION:

What is the Most Important Thing you learned so Far in Business??? :D Yo ;)

3 Rules of Thumb to Increased Happiness

These are the 3 rules that I try to live by:

1. Don't say thank you if you pay for something.

2. Say Thank you if you don't pay for something.

3. Don't make "Your Problem My Problem" also YPMP not a new concept - Newer to Me - Works FUCKING WONDERS

4. If you pay someone, they're not your friend - You are their client. Don't get friends and business mixed up. Cliche - Of FCUKING Course - But FUCKING Happens All The God Damn FUCKING Time

Question:

Which style do you like most??? :D http://is.gd/ZjSayG

Cheers!!! -jamie:D

3 Rules of Thumb to Increased Happiness

1. Don't say thank you if you pay for something.

2. Say Thank you if you don't pay for something.

3. Don't make "Your Problem My Problem" also YPMP not a new concept – Newer to Me – Works FUCKING WONDERS

4. If you pay someone, they're not your friend – You are their client. Don't get friends and business mixed up. Cliche – Of FCUKING Course – But FUCKING Happens All The God Damn FUCKING Time

Question:

Which style do you like most??? 😃 http://is.gd/ZjSayG

Cheers!!! -jamie:D

Necessity Is Key To Creativity (aka How I Created 7 Steps Out of Wage Slavery)

I think the best albums are the ones where the artist is about to be dropped from their record label -

they have one shot -

They say "FUCK IT" I'm Going to Go Out Swinging!!!

Same with Issac Asimov if you look at how the 3 Laws of Robotics were created.

I've said it before the key to creativity is Necessity.

 Question:

Top 3 Favorite Albums of the last month.

Mine:

Bjork - Homogenic

Incubus - Make Yourself

Julieta Venegas - Limon y Sal

5 Business Rules of Thumb after 2 months going solo

<u>Here's my personal 5 Rules of Thumb for business</u>

Only use freelancers that have a phone number (Google Hangout is acceptable in some instances)

Set milestones - i.e. 35% submittal, 50% submittal, 90% submittal, 100% submittal. How I ran Engineering projects - finding that without these milestones - people don't know what's going on, no timeframes (but 100% submittal). I went back and forth with an Indesign Contractor becaus we didn't have milestones and we both respond quickly - I thought "HEY, THIS IS FUCKING GREAT" - But in Reality, project is taking up too much time and not really getting anywhere... Well VERY SLOWLY.

Be clear on what you WANT - I Mean create a legal document in the beginning that spells out EXACTLY what you both will be doing - without this, you start to scope creep, the contractor doesn't deliver what you expect - Just Trust Me, Be clear and explicit in the beginning with exactly what you want.

Do fixed price jobs - Hourly seems great, but the person will stop responding to calls, carry strange hours, be unresponsive - Again, set clear milestones, be very detailed on the scope of the project - And it Will make Your life SOOOOOOO Much Easier.

Hire People Smarter Than you - In designing an eBook I choose a cover designer that was BY FAR More Talented than me in that area, in a Trademark Attorney, the same. These people have really helped push my business further along - They Know What They're doing, they are professionals and THEY ADVISE Based on What People are really doing, on What Really Sells, And How To Really Make Money.

In Conclusion - (I Don't Like This Word) - Be Clear with What you want and what you want of others, set milestones, hire people smarter than you and Your Life Will Be MUCCCCHHHH FUCKING BETTER!!! Yo ;)

Question:

Putting together the Chapters and Chapter Sub-Headings for this book and I think I'm outsmarting myself by being clever instead of reaching/connecting to my ideal reader. Any times you've outsmarted yourself??? :D

Cheers!!! -jamie :D

My New Go-To Drink!!! :D Yo!!! ;D -jamie :D

my new go-to drink - hielo de naranja con chile con miel, chamoy, pimento negro, sal, mas salsa ;D - quizas con una naranja - SO FUCKING GOOD!!! :D

Something different (a Letter to a Friend doing the Impossible – AKA the Living Forrest Gump LOL!!! :D)

What I recommend is writing down on a piece of paper your ideal/perfect/dream life – no detail TOO small. Then take that paper and put it in storage – somewhere where you won't see it. Go about your life – the ideas will still be in your head.

Basically you've just created your compelling vision – now, check out Tamara Price's class on Udemy entitled, "Achieving Your Dreams" – something like that. One of the cornerstones is to believe you can achieve it/believe you are capable of doing it. I'm not convincing you – just believe it in your subconscious mind (Check out HMI Theory of The Mind – for reference).

Again, go about your life – you're creating a new "known" – mixed with your "compelling vision" and you'll have both your "Why" and "Why Not" ☺ Maybe get a trinket to remind yourself – although, its said in Buddhism that this is a form of attachment (Ask Me) – but I have a Green Bracelet (Pulsera) that I wear that just somehow is connected to my subconscious mind that just works for me.

Don't focus on the goal – focus on your feelings/get in touch with your feelings – and be AWARE of how they change – a goal is a limiter unless its attached to a date or amount of money (The more important the stronger the desire to reach it).

I have been rejected so many times on my book, "FUCK YOU: I Won't Do What You Tell Me" but what keeps me going, is I know (or believe) what will happen to me if I don't complete it!!! That feeling sucks – I don't want to feel sucks – so I take action so I don't feel SUCK. Start Making Action Real Today – Live a S.M.A.R.T. Life!!! ☻

Jamie Smith

@withostomy

Author #1 Amazon Bestseller, 7 Steps Out Of Wage Slavery. Smoker, cappuccino addict, 2x speed world record co-holder, birria aficionado.
Editor: @TheRenegadeInc

Photo taken in Northern Baja, Mexico

www.ingramcontent.com/pod-product-compliance
Lightning Source LLC
Chambersburg PA
CBHW020528290526
45786CB00002B/796